About the Author

A born again Pommie who has made Australia his home for over fifty years but still has a place for Yorkshire and is a regular watcher of "The Yorkshire Vet" and his old hometown. He has been a keen sportsman and supports the Aussies passionately.

I Thought They Spoke English

Robin Clive Reed

I Thought They Spoke English

Olympia Publishers
London

www.olympiapublishers.com
OLYMPIA PAPERBACK EDITION

A CIP catalogue record for this title is
available from the British Library.

ISBN: 978-1-80074-626-8

First Published in 2023

Olympia Publishers
Tallis House
2 Tallis Street
London
EC4Y 0AB

Printed in Great Britain

Acknowledgements

Many thanks go to all my extended family and friends who badgered me to keep going over many years to finish this story.

INTRODUCTION

Robin Clive Hepple was born shortly after Mr Hitler had finished demolishing half of the world in a bloodbath that subsequent generations have tried desperately to emulate. His father—Robin's not Hitler's—is unknown to him and that part of his lineage has lapsed into the realms of history. He has made no attempt to research his background and has no wish to do so in the future. He is who he is.

Married with four children, and at the time of writing he has a tribe of grandchildren and great grandchildren with possibly more to follow. His family have enriched his life as well as being a constant source of worry and beautiful distraction. His wife of fifty odd years was, and still is, his childhood sweetheart and the one person who keeps the world turning.

Robin has strong views on the effects that children's environment has on their social, psychological, and physical development. Indeed, he has experienced this in his own life and in the lives of his children and grandchildren. In particular he has one grandchild who, in Robin's opinion, could have been the victim of a system which is too quick to put children into neat little categories without the knowledge or experience to do so. A junior teacher who used a proforma to confirm her diagnosis rather than to make an objective decision and a concurrence by a doctor who prescribed Ritalin as a first course of action could have impacted terribly on the child. Thankfully, the parents, with family support, refused to accept this and with a changed diet and lots of quality time and love the child now has a normal social and academic life.

The reason that this tome was started was to provide his family with some reason, and to help them understand who he is and where he came from. There is an old saying that goes, "You can't make rice pudding from sheep shit." Robin believes that you can! Just don't go there for dinner.

This story is loosely based on the life of Robin Clive Reed (Hepple) but whilst it closely reflects that life it has been tempered and tampered with to protect the guilty

FOREWORD

I don't know at what age it is accepted that we can really remember events in our lives and recount them accurately and with confidence. Those earliest of pictures that we can view with our eyes closed, like some internal and sometimes intermittent DVD, along with the rest of our lives. Perhaps there are early memories locked away in the caverns of our heads which require some trigger to bring them vividly, and at least in part accurately, to life. When I started this adventure into my life, I thought I would barely fill a single chapter with fragmented and isolated incidents. The writing itself became the trigger that I needed, and I soon found that my mind was working faster than I could record the pictures that flooded and overflowed from somewhere in my head.

I have now some idea of who I have become, who I am today. Many "experts" would have us believe that we all have a genetic fingerprint which alone determines who we are and what we will become. I am sure that with many physical characteristics this is true, but I believe that the environment that we are raised in is equally important and it is not sufficient to say, "just like his father". Perhaps the Ritalin mentality is just an "easy out" in many cases. These few chapters are not meant to be critical, however, and so it is sufficient for me to say that I believe that environment has been a major factor in whom I am today. So, I invite you to come with me on a journey through my life as I remember it. It may not be as accurate as others would believe and I don't care.

So, this is my story, and I will write it as I wish. I hope that you the reader will be entertained by it and enjoy the journey as much as I have. Don't mark it as a teacher would by highlighting my poor grammar or syntax, instead feel free to laugh or cry as the story unfolds. If you can do this then I will have received all the gratification that I set out for.

Finally, I would like to say that I regret very little of my life and would wish to change none of it. I could not appreciate love, joy, happiness, and hope had I not experienced despair, disappointment, and sorrow, for how could I tell the difference?

My thanks go to the many people who have made my life a joy and in particular:

My wonderful wife Patricia and my children Margaret, Robyn, Samantha, and Timothy, and their children and their children.

My long lost and found again sister, Joan, and my brother David for helping me with the earliest memories and for being themselves:

Tich Russell who was my first friend.

The Perrott family who took this Pommie under their wings.

John Bailey Hamilton, a friend forever.

And with tongue in cheek, to Lyndon Baines Johnson whose influence got me a wonderful holiday in the then South Vietnam.

CHAPTER ONE

THE FIRST RECOLLECTIONS

On the twenty-one October 1947 Robin Clive Hepple was introduced into this world and I am told, this miracle of human perpetuation took place in a converted air raid shelter in the quaint hamlet of Hacksforth near Bedale in the North Riding of Yorkshire, England. He was the youngest of three children to Mary Dorothy and John Dickson Hepple, the older siblings being Joan Dorothy and David John, aged six and three respectively at the time of this latest monumental happening. I say that "I am told this", because I have found no records of the birth which was to cause untold problems later in life. Those historians amongst you would recognise that date as being Trafalgar Day, which remembers the defeat of the Spanish Armada by the Lord Horatio Nelson. For many years I was reminded of this event for two reasons. Firstly, because I, like many others, mistakenly thought that Nelson had declared his love for midshipman Hardy with those immortal words "Kiss me Hardy" only to learn that he probably said "Kismet Hardy" which was some reference to fate. Secondly and more importantly I remember that event because dear old mater decided to call me Horatio Nelson Hepple, and but for the intervention and good sense of the midwife that is what I would have had to live with. And so, I became Robin Clive, after Robin Hood and Clive of India, who were two more of my dear old mother's historical favourites.

Through my baby years I can only quote those who say that I was angelic and so well behaved. Of course, those who told me this were just a tad biased and my first real memory was one of being terrified of a hot chestnut seller in Sunderland in the northeast of England. By the time that I had achieved my fourth year, my father was no longer there, and my mother was remarried to a chap called Ted for whom she had been doing housekeeping work, or so the story goes. When I say that my father was no longer there, I have in fact no memory of him at all. Who or what sort of person he was remains a mystery to me and no one seemed to want to talk about him, so he just wasn't there, and apart from passing on some physical genetic traits, he has had no influence on my life.

Anyway, after our mam married Ted, we became part of an extended family of about ten children, which was far too many for Ted and Dorothy to handle, and so Joan and David were sent off somewhere and I was to catch up with them later. Ted's eldest children were quite grown up and three of them had gone off to make their own lives. There was some jealousy from my new steprelos and at times I was the brunt of quite spiteful and violent attention from them. Steprelos is a word that I have made up and therefore it is acceptable in this book. I cannot remember any of this and again I am reliant on hearsay. The end result was that I was sent to join David and Joan at Ashbrook Towers in Sunderland which was a "home" or "orphanage" or whatever nice name was used in those days.

I have at last reached a point when I am getting glimpses of what I believe to be recollections. Indeed, the introduction to matters religious is quite vivid and although it might not be totally accurate, I believe it to be close enough. We attended Sunday school each Sunday afternoon and although I can't remember, I believe there was church in the morning. Anyway, we had wonderful stories read to us about this fellow who was able to perform the most amazing tricks. Some people didn't like him very much though, probably because they couldn't do the tricks as well as him. Anyway, they must not have liked him because they killed him. Now I apologise to those of you who may be offended by a four-year-old's assessment of the life of Jesus but that's the picture I recall. All of this was reinforced by we children cutting out pictures and pasting them into our own little book. In particular there were pictures of a chap with rings around his head who never shaved, and had really long hair, and he wore a dress. I don't know if I passed or failed these early religious studies, and they were only glimpses like a torch that doesn't quite work, and you have to keep tapping when it flashes on and off.

There was one after Sunday School incident that is more than just a glimpse although I probably would prefer to not remember it. It was a cold autumn afternoon as we walked home from another cut and paste of the life of Jesus, the streetlights were on but cast only sickly yellow arcs of light around their own poles like a row of miniature lighthouses struggling to reach each other. Leaves that would have been of all colours had we been able to see them before they started their parachute to the ground and turned into a black, slippery carpet under foot. And there, positioned under one of these lights was an old man selling hot chestnuts. His clothes were at best shabby and patched and he was heavily whiskered, with the light causing him to have a halo, just like Jesus. I think back now and realise that England was still suffering from the effects of World War Two, and he was probably eking out an existence for his family. To me he was quite scary even if I didn't understand why, but scary turned into terrifying when David grabbed me by the arm and pulled me towards the chestnut seller saying, "I can get sixpence for a little boy to cook on his fire." I started screaming and pulling away, and the man started to come towards us, waving his arms and shouting. In retrospect he was probably berating David and not wanting to eat me at all, but terrified became totally blind panic stricken and pulling away from David I ran and ran and eventually I must have ended up at Ashbrook Towers or else this story would end here. I still tread carefully on dark autumn afternoons and keep a lookout for hot chestnut sellers.

That is the extent of Sunderland memories and the next that I can recall Joan, David, and I were in another "home" but this time in Newcastle at a big rambling house called Ramle and pronounced "Ramlee."

CHAPTER TWO

MY SECOND HOME

Ramle in Adderstone Crescent, Jesmond, Newcastle Upon Tyne in the northeast of England is now a very well-to-do area and Allan Shearer may even live in the same area today. If I need to elaborate on Allan Shearer, it would be a waste of time. Homes (orphanages) were quite strictly run, almost militarily and I suppose that was by necessity. I think they were called homes as in "homes for children like us." The people in charge of Ramle were a husband-and-wife team by the name of Mr and Mrs Tait and they were known to us as The Master and The Matron. Mr Tait was an ex-policeman and was a tall, immaculately dressed gentleman with a pencil moustache beneath an enormous nose. He was always humming and was what I would expect an army colonel to look like, very stiff upper lip. A chain smoker who rarely spoke and seemed to just materialise instead of entering rooms and he could be intimidating with only his presence. Matron was exactly that, a portly lady who was always administering something or other and she could have been the prototype for the Hattie Jacques character in the "Carry On" movies. She had the hardest of their tasks as I have come to realise that girls have far more puberty problems than boys. Matron would give us medicine from a bottle with a picture of a giraffe on it that tasted like liquorice and also cod liver oil and checked fingernails and hair for things called nits. They had a huge job looking after us all and maintaining the house, although there were other staff for cooking and cleaning.

The house was set on an enormous block with large areas of lawn at the rear, one of which had a full-size tennis court. The very bottom of this huge back yard had old sheds and lots of trees which would shed their leaves in winter, requiring a concentrated effort from everyone to rake them up. We were ordinary kids and would dive into piles of leaves and throw them in the air. To the casual observer it must have looked like a normal household. The house was a two-storey building which could have been purpose designed for an orphanage. Upstairs there were dormitory style bedrooms with bathrooms and toilets, boys segregated from girls, obviously. Downstairs there was a common room, dining room, TV room and a cloakroom not unlike those in schools with wooden benches and hooks to hang raincoats etc. Further in the bowels of Ramle was a cellar for the coal and mixed demons waiting to be let loose on unsuspecting children. All of the areas were very large, and the common room had banks of wooden lockers in which we kept all of our treasures, even though they were not secured and anyone could access all of the lockers. Master and Matron had their own living and office areas, both upstairs and downstairs, and these were out of bounds unless you were summonsed for some indiscretion or other. Each child had an allocated bed space in the upstairs dormitories, and we had allocated jobs to do, including making our own beds and keeping everything tidy. Permission had to be sought to venture outside to play. Church and Sunday school were compulsory as were cubs/scouts or guides. We holidayed at Butlins each year at Ayr in Scotland and the bigger kids intimidated the little ones, and that is what I thought was a normal childhood. Instead of resenting my life and being bitter I was totally content because I didn't know any differently; this was normal! In retrospect we were well-fed, clothed, in good health, and well-educated in all aspects of schooling and self-discipline. School was my link with reality, and I learned to learn and excelled at sports. As with most boys I adored NUFC (Newcastle United Football Club), refer again to Allan Shearer, and still follow their fortunes to this day.

Our daily routine started with everyone getting up at the appointed time, but I have no idea what that time was except it was the same every day. I'm sure that I must have understood the concept of time however I cannot remember having to know what time it was that I did anything. I simply responded to a series of stimuli and orders in the required way and as often as possible in the right sequence. Anyway, after getting dressed, and I somehow knew what to wear, it was wash hands and face and present for breakfast. In the dining room we all had our allocated place at the table and would stand there until allowed to be seated. There was a quick prayer of thanks and everyone on a given signal would sit, with no scraping of chairs, and eat in silence or at least as silently as a room full of children could eat. There were no seconds, nor would any be left because it was a sin to waste good food. I never got a definition of "good food." Again, on the given signal, we would collectively stand up, with no scraping of chairs, and file out to the kitchen with our plates and cutlery. Then it was jobs, school, or whatever else we were directed to do. Afternoons it was homework, jobs, a repeat of breakfast, but without the porridge and if we were lucky an hour of television before bath and bed. Television was one of the great benefits of life in a "home" and by the mid-fifties we could savour the delights of "The Cisco Kid", "The Lone Ranger", and other classic westerns when the good guys wore white, the bad guys black and we always knew who would win. And who could forget

PC Dixon of Dock Green as he stood under the station light and whilst rocking gently on the balls of his feet he would utter those immortal words, "Evenin' all." In years to come PC Dixon would re-emerge in my life as a police sergeant with size ten boots. My grandchildren are fascinated that as a five-year-old I watched "Basil Brush" and they are in awe when I speak of "Sooty" and "The Flowerpot Men." Then it was wash or bath and into bed with no talking. For at the slightest giggle the Master would materialise and with only a changed pitch in his humming there was a silence that was deafening until he once more disappeared like smoke in a stiff breeze. Bath night would offer some variation to the routine, as we were paraded by gender and age to bathe and towel dry under strict supervision. No chance of any peeking at the girls in that place and so the fundamental difference between the sexes eluded me for many years to come. My life meandered through the caverns and gorges of my time at Ramle, and this disciplined and regimented way of life became the normal. A total lack of emotional stimuli was punctuated only by the simple joys of warm summer evenings when we were allowed outside to play or the regular but spasmodic events that broke the monotony. I had not realised it yet but there was now two of me; one who lived in the home and one who lived outside the home.

One of those regular out of the home events was the annual holiday to Butlins at Ayr in Scotland. Butlins Holiday Camps could be best described as organised holidays for those people who find it difficult to enjoy themselves without an instruction manual and someone to read and interpret it. The hint is not in the "holiday" element but rather the "camp" element. The ride to Ayr was to my memory by train but my big sister advises that it was by bus. In any event it was a magical journey as we passed through farmland that looked like huge jigsaw puzzles and through quaint villages with unpronounceable names with houses that would surely fall over in a good wind. They were probably held up by the ivy and other growth that covered all of them so that only tiny doors and windows peeked out from their sides and smoky chimneys from the roofs. Arriving in Ayr we were greeted by a bagpipe band in full regalia. They produced a sound that I have in later years heard someone replicate, albeit quite cruelly, by placing a cat under their armpit and biting its tail. After alighting or debussing, if I believe my big sister, we were allocated to "houses" much the same as in school, for the duration of the holiday. The reason for this was so that everyone would know which sitting you would go to for meals and which activities to attend. All of this is controlled by people known as Redcoats which was no doubt to hide the bloodstain caused by rebelling campers in the tradition of the English Army in such actions as the Zulu Wars. After allocation we were shown to our chalets, which were a series of semi-detached wooden huts with beds and some basic furniture like a table and chair so that we could send compulsory postcards to our loved ones that we didn't know and tell them what a marvellous place this was and how much we are enjoying it. Soon it's our turn for lunch in the dining complex, which is strangely similar to an army mess hall. And can you imagine the looks on the faces of fellow campers as we stand waiting for the word to sit and give thanks for the food. The spell is broken by someone announcing over the speaker system that there will be a tug-of-war competition on the grassed area adjacent to the gymnasium at one-thirty sharp. Please move to that area for team allocations. I hadn't eaten lunch yet and we are into the holiday activities. This is truly home away from "The Home", with no need to think, just follow instructions. This is a well thought out holiday destination. And so, we arrive at the tugging destination and are allocated into teams. Not having any fat kids, we put Horace Georgeson as our anchor so if the other team pulled really hard it would be him that was torn in half as we all let go of the rope. Horace was an easy touch and not the full quid. Anyway, we tugged off (not my terminology), for the rest of the day and the victors got their score on the board in the dining area so that they could gloat over breakfast. Which reminds me, although it may be traditionally Scottish, I can assure you that their porridge was ghastly, and I think it was made with sea water and sheep manure.

One of the most vivid memories of Butlins at Ayr was another frightening experience and one that still haunts me to this day. In our spare time we were allowed to play in the pool in our black woolly swimmers that came up to our midriffs and accentuated the ghostly white of our scrawny bodies and irritated any skin unfortunate enough to come into contact with them. This in itself was heaps of fun as we splashed around in two foot six inches of a chemical/urine solution with gay abandonment. That is until the inevitable competition, which was naturally swimming. To allocate teams we were lined up along the side of the pool and had to swim to the other side. To be fair there may have been some attempt to identify non swimmers but unless told otherwise I would just stand where I was told and jump in when I was told and that is what happened. I don't know who pulled me out but to this day I get tight in the chest in deep water and am not a strong swimmer. My family say that I dive like a duck and swim like a brick. But don't worry, it gets better and remember that I was totally insulated against this because it was "normal".

And so, the Butlins experience was played out each year and

each year we sent postcards to people we didn't know to tell them what a wonderful time we were having and then it was back to Ramle and the safety of our routine life and everything was as it should be with the Redcoats, the bagpipes, and the competitions forgotten for another year.

There is a time each year when we celebrate a religious festival that should be a magical event for all children. Life at Ramle was no different when, in the midst of winter with the snow drifting and snowmen appeared with their carrot noses, old pipes, and stick arms, we would celebrate Christmas. For us children it was extra special because up until the very day we didn't even know that it was Christmas. The routines hadn't changed and up until porridge being devoured and the plates cleared away nothing special had occurred. Then we were ushered into the common room to be greeted with piles of treasures laid out in neat rows, one pile beside each locker, and there we would stand and wait for Master and Matron to materialise. The excitement was unbearable to the point that I would almost wet my pants but I wouldn't leave my pile for fear that the older children would steal something. Matron would be saying something about charitable and generous gifts donated by blah, blah, blah, and whatever else she said. Then it was, "You can open your gifts now", followed by a mad ripping and tearing of the green and gold paper. The charitable organisations were indeed generous and soon we were all absorbed in toys and sweets and clothes. This was followed by screams of "it's got a real bell" each dashing to someone else's toys to look in wonderment at their treasure. We played and ate sweets and pushed the clothes to one side until Master would interject with, "Time to pick up all the paper and clean up. Everyone put your things in your lockers and carry on with your allocated jobs." I was in awe imagining all the kids in the world standing beside their lockers after breakfast on Christmas day and I wondered what magical signal was given for the opening of presents that must have happened at the same time everywhere in the world.

There were other fine things about Christmas though, like the wondrous tree that appeared overnight on the landing at the top of the stairs, and we paraded past it with eyes so wide that the baubles, lights, and tinsel were reflected like our own laser light show whilst a huge angel looked over us. And there were decorations that again just appeared magically and fluttered and rotated on their cotton anchors with the occasional balloon exploding to startle even the Master and he would stop humming momentarily. Even the midday meal was transformed into a feast with roasted vegetables and apple sauce on our meat. Some of the crackers exploded with a puff of gunpowder whilst others just fizzed and spilled their contents onto the table, and we all put on our paper hats, and unlike normal meals we were allowed to not only talk but were encouraged to laugh and call out with glee at our good fortune. The pudding was covered in thick rich custard and contained threepenny and sixpenny pieces, although we had to keep them to one side as they would be used next year. I didn't believe this as I thought the cook kept them as a Christmas bonus. After lunch we were allowed to go to Jesmond Dene with sledges and fly down the snow-covered paths until we reached the little bridge at the bottom and we had competitions to see who could get over that humpy little structure and run down the snowmen on the other side. They were funny little structures with carrot noses, stone eyes and stick arms, and they never totally went away but rather slowly developed midriff bulges and their heads gradually sank to the ground and merged with the slush. Christmas Day ranked second to no other day in the calendar but there were things missing that I still cannot remember, no matter how hard I try or under what conditions, for instance, there was never a person called Santa Claus, there were no cards from loving aunties, uncles, or grandparents, and the presents were never at the end of the bed, which is something that my children cannot understand, even today.

For weeks, the Master would, with assistance from all sorts of weird people, gather cart loads of old trees and wood, car tyres, furniture, cardboard, and anything else that would burn, and make a huge bonfire at the bottom of the garden. The pile was as tall as a house and sitting on top was a scarecrow that I later learned was an effigy of a chap named Guy Fawkes who hatched a plan to blow up some place called the Houses of Parliament on November the fifth a long time ago. And so, we have those famous words, "Remember, remember the fifth of November, gunpowder, treason and plot." It mattered not about Mr Fawkes, the only thing that I cared about was the day that the bonfire was lit, and the flames danced up to the trees and made them shiver and tremble, and the scarecrow would slowly disintegrate and fall into the flames sending showers of sparks which rivalled the fireworks display that would follow soon after.

We were warned, "Stand back and be very careful" and then, "Stay rugged up and away from the fire", and a constant stream of warnings to ensure our safety, which for me were totally unnecessary because I was transfixed as rockets flew skywards only to reappear in a cascade of coloured lights that disappeared before they reached earth, and left that wonderful smell that only fireworks night can generate, and that stays with you for at least two days, especially if bath night wasn't straight away. There were Catherine Wheels that spun on wooden boards, Roman Candles which showered like volcanoes of coloured sparks into the air, and the Jumping Jacks and Bungers that made Matron scream and berate the Master or whoever almost certainly threw them with the sole purpose of threatening her wellbeing, and they all laughed and so did we. All too soon it was over, and we were all tucked into our beds, but sleep would not come quickly as the magnificent display was played over and over in our heads and we giggled at the memory of Matron's screaming and yelling at the Master.

These were some of the occasions that punctuated the monotony of my everyday disciplined routine life where days blended into weeks, months, and years. They were the events that made everything have a reason and were eagerly awaited and then lost as quickly as they arrived. There were some parts of the daily routines however that also were eagerly awaited and savoured as much as any of the special days because they were outside days.

I played football (soccer) for my school team from the age of five, and although I say so myself, I was very good at it and my ambition even then was to play football for Newcastle United when I grew up. Because I was so football mad, I was taken to St James' Park on some Saturday afternoons to watch the "Toon" play, the Toon being what Geordies call their football team. The crowds were huge, possibly a million in my mind, and the noise deafening as the black and white clad players jogged onto the pitch. If the opposition played well, they would get a reluctant and subdued applause, but when Newcastle attacked, looked dangerous, or scored, then the noise could be heard at any other place that existed on earth, but I didn't know about. I assumed then that I would still be in Ramle well into adulthood and football would be my escape route to normality, whatever that was. The kit that we wore in those days was of course not the same as the flash advertising hoardings worn by today's players but rather more heavy-duty clothes with leather boots that came past the ankles with leather studs nailed to the sole that wore down at every different angle to make walking almost impossible on concrete before they were replaced. But I always felt as though I was running out for the "Toon" with a large black number five in a white square on the back of my shirt to indicate that I was the centre half. In those days, all teams played with the numbers one to eleven on their shirts, unlike today when numbers relate more to your transfer date rather than your playing position. All the great centre forwards wore the number nine like Milburn and Clough. But not the nine for me, for I would be that centre of defence that would prevent goals and so, on the town common each Saturday the best player for West Jesmond Junior School was Robin Hepple, and I played my very best to ensure that each week it was me in that number five shirt and not the inside me sitting in the common room doing nothing exciting.

As soon as I was old enough, I was enrolled into Cubs and this became another eagerly awaited outside activity that was pursued with the utmost effort to ensure that it became a regular event. Badges became an obsession to obtain and so I practiced tying knots, learning chants and everything else, except swimming which I still shied away from, and soon became a Seconder and then a Sixer which is like a Cubs Section Commander. Jamborees, bivouacs, weekend collections and Bob A Job Week were opportunities to escape the boredom and monotonous existence of life at Ramle. Again, I was blissfully unaware that sports, cubs/scouts, and school were to be of the greatest value to me later in life when I would have to use these self-disciplinary skills to their fullest effect.

My family to this point consisted of my older siblings Joan

and David and those people ensconced in Ramle. On occasions someone would mention "your mother" but this was some mythical person who had no place in my life or in any memories of life before the "homes." Of course she was undoubtedly a real person, it was just that I had no recognition of her and that included photographs or even a verbal description from Joan or David. If they had talked of her, then I either didn't listen or could not comprehend their explanations.

The day had to arrive when I would be confronted with this mythical person and would therefore need to adjust my youthful beliefs of who I was and where I came from, and not in the physical sense of childbirth. When the day did arrive there was a total feeling that I should be excited and run to her and fold into her ample bosom and melt into a wonderful place of comfort and safety. She was "me mam". And the day did arrive and she did come to visit her children at Ramle. We were forewarned of her impending arrival and had I been intelligent enough then our pre visit briefing would have been exposed as the need for our Master and Matron to ensure that no indiscreet mention should be made of anything bad that had happened. They need not have worried, if indeed they did, for Joan was excited to see our mam, David was never as happy as he was at Ramle anyway, and I was scared of anything or anyone outside of my little world.

The first visit, indeed the only visit that I can recall, was so traumatic that I was distressed by the time she arrived. She was an "old" person to me although probably only in her early thirties and I thought her to be quite beautiful, which only added to my reluctance to be close to her. She had fair mousy coloured hair which had obviously been in curlers for some time. Her skin was quite white and she wore little or no makeup and was dressed in a summery frock down to just below her knees, carried her handbag on one forearm and seemed to walk a little bit like a duck. This may appear to be a fairly in-depth description for a young boy but I was entranced by her and stared incessantly, unable to do the hugging things that Joan and David seemed to be doing as naturally as breathing. I may be biased in my recollection of her because later in life she was always dressed and looked the same as that day.

We walked around at Jesmond Dene, and she was no doubt trying very hard to get my approval and kept pinching my cheeks and calling me "Her little Robin". I know that we went to a café, and she bought us "bangers and mash" and this was probably the closest she was going to get in winning my approval. It was, no doubt, a most heart-breaking time for her, with Joan happy to see her, David just busting to get back to Ramle, and me pulling away from her every time she tried to hug me or get into my space. At the end of the day, she went to wherever it was she had to go and we went back to the safety of the Home and I felt that this woman was a nice lady but still a total stranger to me.

By the time I was ten years old there was a resignation in me that this was normal even though other children at school and cubs/scouts told of things that they did with their mams and das. Newcastle in the fifties was a fairly drab place and I could always tell other kids of our Butlins holidays and church and cubs and football. They probably thought I had rich parents who didn't have to disguise the Sunday roast with puddings and gravy on the piece of grisly tough meat and that I was always well dressed and had all the right school equipment. I was doing quite well really!

CHAPTER THREE

WELCOME TO MALTKILN COTTAGES

The season, day, and time totally elude me, but the reactions of my siblings and I will stay with me forever when we were told that we were going home. Had the whole world gone crazy; this was home, how could we go there when we were already there! David, who is an epileptic, fitted on the spot, I cried uncontrollably, I think for the first time in my life, and Joan had already left to live with grandparents in Sunderland. I was akin to a long-term prisoner who was being released into a world that they could not possibly understand but had for so long craved. How could these people who had ruled my life so completely now abandon me and hand me over to complete strangers without so much as a by-your-leave? I also have no idea how we got from Ramle to Maltkiln Cottages in Thirsk, Yorkshire, except for the train ride which we completed unchaperoned, and I remember passing from the grey industrial northeast to expanses of fields and clear, clean air and skies that looked to be so much higher than in Newcastle. One thing that was for sure and certain is that my life totally changed during the next five years.

As it turned out we didn't go to live with our mother and stepfather, Ted, but rather we became our own little family group living in close proximity to Mam and Step Dad. What had happened was that the firm that Ted worked for had built two semidetached houses for the foreman and leading hand at the

Maltkiln, which had left the old cottages empty. Two of my stepsisters and their partners occupied two of the old cottages and Joan, David, myself, and an old gentleman, who turned out to be my grandfather on my mother's side, got the third. Your impeccable maths will now tell you that two houses were built but three old ones were occupied; the third had been occupied by an old lady who had lived there for perhaps four hundred years as far as I could ascertain, until she had recently passed away, and this was to be our old cottage. I immediately hated this place but not for any logical or real reason other than it was not the safe haven that had been my life to date. This wonderful two-storey cottage brought back a vague memory from when I was part of the newly formed family after Mam remarried. I cannot remember how it happened, but my stepsister Vera had evidently lashed out with a comb which left me with a gash under my left eye, the scar from which I still bear, and we had lived in one of these cottages then. Grandfather was evidently to fill the role of father, Joan the mother, and David and I the children with extra parental support from mam and step-father just down the road. It was a recipe for disaster and was destined never to work.

Grandfather Hoggar, my mother's maiden name evidently, was probably one hundred and fifty years old at this time with pronounced jowls, wispy grey hair, spectacles, and smelled like what I thought an old man should smell like, all musty and damp. My grandchildren will not know this smell, I hope. He never actually talked to us but rather mumbled and blew his breath out in gusts from swollen cheeks through the corners of his mouth and as such I never really knew what to do or say around him. He wasn't the formidable presence of the Master and he shuffled rather than strode straight-backed and I will probably look just like him one day. Joan was about sixteen by now and had finished a Secretarial Course through school in Newcastle and I would imagine that the responsibility of being mother to David and I was quite daunting, especially with Mam and Ted monitoring events from a short distance away. Anyway, she found work in Thirsk as a secretary to the manager of a car firm which was part of the Rootes Group, which distributed such vehicles as the Humber range. The short and turmoil-filled period, lasted only months before it all fell apart, and once again I was relocated, although this time only just down the road.

I have no idea in retrospect how anyone could have imagined that this domestic arrangement could have worked. A sister trying to be mother, a grandfather trying to be father, and two brothers who wanted to be somewhere else was indeed a recipe for disaster and I wonder if anyone had actually thought this through or if it was simply a good way to get us out of the "home" either for financial reasons or from some actual consideration for we children.

As I mentioned, Joan had found work as a secretary to the manager of the Rootes Group car sales. With the luxury of hindsight, the name should have been setting off alarm bells for within a short period of time she had rushed off to the Midlands with the manager to seek a better life away from Thirsk. I never felt let down by this or angry in any way because I knew that she had escaped a life that had been a millstone around her neck and even though it would be a long time before she found true happiness this was the breakaway that she had desperately needed. In the short time that Joan had been my "mother" I found a love for her that I hold dear to this day. I am often asked if I want to go back to visit the UK and I answer honestly that my only wish would be to see Joan before one or both of us pass on. In retrospect she was the closest I came to a mother figure ever.

She was the one who made my breakfast and prepared me for school and made sure that my hair was combed and teeth brushed. She was the one who applied first aid if I grazed a knee, and she was the one who got angry at me if I stayed out late in the summer months playing football in the field behind the pub. She didn't have all the skills, but she more than made up for it with care and affection. She even took me to the pictures with one of her boyfriends, which probably didn't happen often with big sisters and little brothers.

Grandfather Hoggar grunted and shuffled his way through the short period of our relationship, and I cannot remember him having a single input into my lifestyle other than his presence. He was grumpy at best and I suppose he didn't really enjoy this time either as he had already raised his family and wanted to live his life of retirement in peace and quiet doing whatever old folks did then. Anyway, he either just got sick of the arrangement or he genuinely got too old and was shipped off to an old people's home. His story doesn't quite end there however as he once again found love and shagged himself to death in the old folks' home, so one of us found happiness even if it was short lived. As they say, they couldn't get the smile off his face or the coffin lid shut at his funeral. David spent a short period arguing with Mam and Ted and anyone who would argue with him. I heard that he had "run-away" and was working at Northallerton and had found digs there. He would visit me from time to time and we would sing songs to radio Luxemburg, and he would tell of the wonderful life that he had, and then off he went again on the train to Northallerton, and I never visited him there. He had a job preparing bodies in the morgue at the Northallerton Hospital, which I could never come to grips with and never saw it being a wonderful vocation but rather a morbid existence. This left me, and of course I couldn't stay there by myself and so I went to live with Mum and Ted, my stepbrother David, and half-brother Francis. Mum and Ted had added to the family numbers with Francis who was six years younger than me, and probably at the age when they had decided to send me to Ramle. Thankfully, that didn't happen to Francis and he lived at home until his tragic death on his eighteenth birthday. David Reed was the last of Ted's children to live at home and he was doing an apprenticeship as a chippy or builder or something like that and we developed a love/hate relationship in that we loved to hate each other and I dreamed of the day that I would be big enough to retaliate without getting beaten up. I have to be honest and say that the older we got the less antagonistic we became, to the point where we would speak to each other, and I accepted him as a big brother figure. I had a limited number of jobs to do and the freedom to come and go as I pleased, didn't have to go to church or Sunday School, and within reason no curfews to observe.

Having not to ask permission to go outside and gaining the freedom that this brought meant, of course, that I abused the privilege to the maximum but never seemed to get disciplined for staying out playing football or sitting precariously atop an old railway carriage trainspotting or starting a collection of bird's eggs, as long as the coke was in each day, and I escorted Ted to Buffaloes each second Friday. Yes, everything was cool and I set about cramming as much outside time into the next few years as I possibly could.

At this point I should explain just where it was that this took place. On the edge of the Yorkshire moors is a small town with a rather famous racecourse and it is surrounded by many smaller villages on roads that lead to other towns. The town is called Thirsk and we lived a little way out of town at Thirsk Junction at which point the main north/south railway line passes. Thirsk is not unlike hundreds of small English towns with a central cobblestone marketplace which is full of stalls with every imaginable produce each market day. In the centre of the marketplace is the bus terminal with a large tower with four clocks in it and the four roads out of or into town culminate at the bus stop. All of the business houses surround the marketplace with their small bells attached to their doors and musty smells and old-fashioned wares and they all appear to have old world facades hiding dingy back rooms where their owners live. And there are many pubs with charming names like "The Farmers Arms", "The Fox and Hounds", and "The Old Red House". These old pubs are full of atmosphere and probably attract tourist dollars today, but then for the locals they were meeting places to discuss the important issues of the day such as the price of potatoes, the new tractor and what their team did right or wrong on Saturday. Each of the roads out of town passes through villages until the next town, and we lived on the road that passed the racecourse and the railway station and on to Carlton Minniott, the small village with the Junior School. Along the road were rows of terraced houses, with some new bungalows and fields with rows of potatoes, turnips, or dairy cows lazily grazing in fields separated by tall hedges interrupted by rickety wooden gates, and there were Ferguson tractors with ploughs or muddy trailers, and the smell of the country air was intoxicating. Opposite the railway station was the Maltkiln that Ted was foreman of and of course the New Maltkiln Cottages in which I now lived. This was all mine to explore and become intimate with over the next few years and I was to learn about every square inch of this paradise.

I went to school at the little Carlton Minniott school with

about thirty primary school children from kindergarten to pre-secondary modern ages all contained in one large room with two teachers. My time here was a doddle because the enforced learning in Newcastle had left me well ahead of the other children, which I say not in a bragging way but simply as a matter of fact. It was to prove more of a hindrance than a help later because I turned off and didn't start the learning process until I realised that they had not only caught up but indeed passed me and then I really needed to knuckle down. Whilst the numbers were small, the diversification of kids was huge with the really poor ones with patched clothes and constantly runny noses, the rich farmers' kids with leather satchels and pocket money, the bully and the bullied, the comedian, and the rest of us who came somewhere in the middle. I was probably not really in the middle but in a group of my own with very few social skills, until I palled up with Brian 'Tich' Russell. Tich lived in the railway cottages with his parents and siblings and he was to become the closest that I have ever come to a best friend until then. We shared a passion for football and spent hundreds of hours with two coats on the ground for goals and taking it in turns to be goalkeeper. We developed our own rhyming slang with phrases such as "second-hand shop" for a second time shot and we would alternatively be the greatest players of the day such as Brian Clough or Lev Yashin the Russian goalkeeper. And when we weren't kicking a football, we were just roaming around the countryside collecting bird's eggs or skimming rocks or just being friends. I had truly found the friend that a young boy needed, but when I left Thirsk, I didn't get the opportunity to say goodbye to him which is one of the things I regret.

One of my few chores was to escort Ted to his Buffalo Meetings. He had a glass eye and couldn't see the curb when riding his bicycle. I would ride on his outside, and if he kept away from me, we would do OK. Going to the pub was easy but returning could be traumatic as he was not sober. With cars tooting their horns and him wobbling everywhere, the inevitable happened and somehow, he ended up in some rose bushes. Amidst much *** and suffering he extracted his bloodied form and I swear that none of this was intentional on my behalf, although I was severely punished for it.

I passed the exams to get into Grammar School which was simply the 'A' stream of the Secondary Modern School and travelled to the school some three miles away on foot until I got my job as a paper boy and then rode the big red paper bike to school. I enjoyed school in the same way as in Newcastle, and once I had realised that I needed to work harder I had the self-discipline to do what was required. Homework was the hardest because there was always something to do, but it always got done and I started to believe that I might "make something of myself" as my mother would often plead. There was never any monitoring of school work or homework and never any offer of assistance or reading of school reports. In fact, I cannot remember any real parent/son type of communication and I didn't try to instigate any.

CHAPTER FOUR

THE FREEDOM TO DO

There were an endless number of things to explore and learn in this new environment and having a fellow kid to do it with made them even more exciting. Guy Fawkes night was one of the highlights of Ramle, but it paled into insignificance compared to the fifth of November in Thirsk. The thrill of watching became the thrill of doing. Making the bonfire was the responsibility of everyone in the area and the range of combustible material was absolutely endless, suffice to say if it burned it was used. Remember that in those days there was no such thing as environmental restrictions, so tyres, waste oils, plastics and the like were used. This building process would go on for weeks before the big day and the bonfire would reach huge proportions in the field behind The Railway pub.

Something that was new to me was the tradition of "mischief night" on the fourth of November when it was tolerated that we kids could get up to some harmless mischief, if there is such a thing. Fireworks had been on sale for several weeks so we were fully prepared with Jumping Jacks, Rockets and of course Penny Bungers (later Threepenny Bungers). And so, the night would start with bungers in forty-four-gallon drums and other enclosed containers such as steel pipes and then with four tied together before we moved on to the real stuff. In those days houses had slots in their front doors with spring-loaded flaps so that mail and newspapers could be delivered and the clever people made sure that on this night they were jammed shut. For those that didn't the night was about to get fairly ordinary as mischief gave way to stupidity. A handful of soap powder in a small box with a bunger in it pushed through a letter box shortly after lighting would scare the living daylights out of the occupants and leave powder and cardboard everywhere. The next "clever" idea was to put dog poo in a large paper bag, knock on a door and light the bag, causing the occupant to stamp on the bag when they got to the door. The mischief turned into vandalism and we roared with laughter as we ran off after putting honey and feathers on someone's car windscreen and angry citizens shook their fists and called us the names that although were fairly vulgar were also fairly apt. And so, mischief night was high on the list of topics being discussed by the populace next morning, and the reason for the local bobby visiting certain households to administer size ten justice. Mischief night was officially retracted from the calendar but took forever to actually end.

Nothing could stop the big night however and as dark descended the bonfire was lit and would slowly lick and dance its way to the summit, and then slowly spread to become an inferno, and even the smoke blended every different colour into the dense black toxic swirl. Fireworks of every sort would be going off from every direction with showers of coloured sparks, and overhead the rockets exploded with their own explosions of colour and smoke trails. This time though I was setting the fireworks off with my own box of matches, and the only injury that I can remember was stepbrother David having a bunger go off in his pocket when trying to scare his sister Vera, and at that time I thought this was more funny than tragic, but I was biased. Potatoes were cooked in the hot coals and the grownups sat around drinking whatever it was that made them talk absolute rubbish and laugh a lot and fall over a lot. At some time, I went to bed and again the smell of fireworks hung in the air like an autumn mist and I couldn't sleep for fear of forgetting the night's events.

Christmas never reached the heights of Ramle. I asked for and received either a football or football boots each year, if we had a Christmas tree, I can never remember it, nor the decorations, and the snow was either feet deep or just slush. I even thought of getting a locker in my shared bedroom, but stepbrother David would have booby trapped it and Ted wouldn't have had any idea why it was there, and he probably wouldn't have known the universal signal to open presents. And so, Christmas lost its glitz and apart from the school nativity, cards from obscure people, and Tich telling me what it was all about for him, I never really enjoyed Christmas until I left Thirsk. I'm glad that I learned before I had children of my own. The only new thing that Christmas bought was the carol singers who went from street to street with mixed responses from the residents. Some applauded and donated money for whatever the cause (perhaps that was how Ramle got their donations), others hurled abuse and some actually threw things at them, like buckets of water. I always enjoyed the singers and would join in when they were at Maltkiln Cottages, and then follow them until some ratbag would be abusive, when I would take off. Throughout all of the festive season there was still the freedom to come and go as I liked.

One of the freedoms that I had was the option of either going or not going to church and Sunday school. I chose not to, simply because I believed that there were far better things to do on Sundays and also because none of my friends or Mam and Ted went. I have never felt that I am an atheist because of non-attendance at church, although the Reverend Crossley tried very hard to convince me otherwise when I went to be married sometime later. In those days when so many new adventures beckoned, the idea of wasting time seemed to be so stupid. How could church compete with long walks in the country, climbing trees, fishing, riding our pushbikes, and just hanging out with those people who were now my life? I will admit however that the thought of going to church has often crossed my mind throughout my life and my religious teaching has always remained strong in my memory, and I would never be critical of anyone's beliefs as long as they remained theirs and made no attempt to convert me.

During my time at Thirsk, football was still a huge part of my life. I couldn't go to see my beloved Newcastle United, but Tich and I would often go to Middlesbrough to watch the "Boro" play at Ayresome Park. We caught the train to Darlington and changed for the coast train to Middlesbrough or simply caught a bus for the whole journey. Sitting in the stands and cheering the Boro was as exciting as being at St James' Park, and we both ended up hoarse and worn out, and could talk for hours afterwards replaying every minute, and if the manager could take our comments on board the team might have won the First Division (the Premier League didn't exist then). The only player that we didn't try to improve on was Brian Clough because even we couldn't improve on perfection.

There is a trend in today's world for the younger generation to be bored and they cannot find anything to entertain themselves unless it is purchased or given to them. I thought it a crime to waste even one minute of free time and cannot remember being bored at any time that I was in Thirsk. Even exploring in the Maltkiln was exciting and there were always trees to climb, fields to explore, bicycle rides, footballs to be kicked, and a thousand other ways to fill in hours without needing any electronic devices or bought toys.

Those of you who can remember the days of steam engines and the character that they exuded will still marvel at those mammoths of the transport world. I was lucky enough to live during those days and even luckier to be able to feel the house shake as they passed at full tilt and no more than one hundred yards away. The main north/south line meant that we were able to sit for hours atop an unused railway sawdust carriage and "train spot". Tich and I and Bas Foster and Fish Hardy and anyone else who could fit on the carriage could while away hours writing down all the numbers from all of the trains that passed and feel the exhilaration of the van shaking from the vibrations of those monsters as they rocked and rattled along the tracks. We sat in silence awaiting the tell-tale sound of steel on steel followed by a shrill whistle in the distance as the train announced its arrival, and then the shaking would start and it slowly became more pronounced until our lofty perch shook violently, and the train sped passed with smoke bellowing from its stack to dissipate first clear and then grey and then black and then gone with only the coal smell left and another number to write down. Sometimes I was so engrossed in watching the train and marvelling at the engineering brilliance that I wouldn't write down the number and Tich would make me grovel before he gave it to me. Often in the passenger trains we got waves and other gestures from the occupants and I wondered where they were going and what purpose they had on this earth. Each class of locomotive had their own distinguishing features such as the number of wheels, the streamlining, the positioning of the stack and even some with blinkers on like steeplechase horses at the racecourse. Each one had its own number and these could be crossed out in a Train Spotters Book and we would compare the numbers that we had, especially any that were rare or hard to get. We bragged often about such things as "I got this 2-10-0 at Harrogate when we visited Auntie Flo", or "This 0-6-0 was shunting here yesterday." All of the trains were fascinating but the ones that left an absolute tingle down the spine were the A4 Pacific speedsters that almost pulled us off our carriage like some huge magnet that wanted to drag us to its destination. I cannot remember how many of these streamlined beauties there where but one in particular was the "Mallard" with its plaque all polished to announce that it was the holder of the steam train speed record in all the world, and when its blue bullet-like body proudly sped down the line we all wrote down the number 4468 once again. There is no doubt those amongst you who would say that the death of the steam locomotive was a triumph for environmental longevity and that they were smoke billowing filthy things left over from some prehistoric time when no one cared about the ozone layer being eroded. We were blissfully unaware of the environmental repercussions and only saw steam trains as another source of entertainment, besides which I doubt that they were any worse than the diesel monstrosities that were to take their place or the escalation of our roads to accommodate the ever-increasing volume of motor traffic. However, the inevitable happened just before I left Thirsk and Dogface Diesels started to trundle along the lines and steam trains were being phased out.

Many of the things that we did to prevent boredom were, in retrospect, either plain stupid or even illegal, and for the latter reason I will refrain from recounting some of them, for although the repercussions are probably not going to be severe, I don't particularly want anyone to know how all those railway shed windows, were broken, or why I was in the Maltkiln with Ted's binoculars. There were however some which deserve some expansion in this forum. Collecting birds' eggs was fairly popular in this era and although the number of eggs collected was relatively small, the collection part was always good fun and often quite dangerous. We would walk in the countryside for hours scanning the trees and waterways and fields for nests. Once located, the fun part started in trying to reach the nest. Hanging from branches whilst the one on the ground gave instructions was at best silly and at worst dangerously stupid, but youngsters didn't then and don't now seem to grasp this. If the nest could be reached, then one egg only would be removed if it was from a type that we didn't have, as we thought that we were being like conservationists by only taking one egg. I later realised that robbing nests cannot be condoned no matter how good the intention, but it was good fun then. Birds are clever little things and often build their nests in places that are just out of reach like in the eaves of tall buildings and on that floating vegetation that means you have to fall into five feet of water or stand in two feet of mud to get to them. The end result was that the birds more often than not won and our collections could be captured in one cotton wool filled shoe box. The other really good part about collecting eggs was that you got to blow them which is a term used to remove the white and yolk through two small pin holes at either end of the egg. We needed to practice this art and would do so with eggs borrowed from Ted's chicken run. Take the egg and with a needle, pierce each end of the shell and then blow through one of these holes until all of the egg's contents is out, then return the egg to the chicken run. It is one thing that Ted never caught me for!

Now there are some adults who simply cannot stand kids and will do anything that they can to chase, harass, and generally verbally abuse them. So was the case with one old chap in Railway Terrace who spent a large portion of his time-consuming Scotland's finest, annoying kids, and tending his vegetable garden. "You young'uns got no respect", or "If I catch yer I'll kick yer arses and tell yer das on yer" and other such threats were common in his relationship with the youth of Thirsk Junction. Of course all of his tirades were unprovoked in any way and we never annoyed him at all. And so, this running war of words went on until one day he clipped Sid Calvert on the back of his head and Sid bawled his eyes out. I should point out that Sid was physically challenged and as is the way with young boys, he was never part of the team but rather just hung around with everyone else. This however bonded him to the team, in fact I believe that he would have gladly copped a flogging every day to be part of the group. Sid had given us the right to retaliate and so we did his vegetable garden over. At the time it seemed like a fair thing to do but of course in hindsight it was malicious and I deserved everything I got as retribution. By the time I got home the local bobby was waiting for me and with one ear firmly held between thumb and forefinger he proceeded to plant his size ten onto my buttocks several times whilst I apologised and swore never to do anything like this again, and that I would immediately repair the damage and replace the vegetables. This achieved, it was Ted's turn to administer much the same whilst I promised much the same, and then the worst part as Mam went on and on about trying to bring me up knowing right from wrong and blah, blah, blah, until Ted gave me another clip under the ear and suggested that she shut up. All of this would seem fairly brutal to today's educated child experts but if instant punishment which is not physically scarring were able to be meted out today then some louts would think twice. As for not understanding right from wrong, I can assure you I always knew when I had stuffed up and the consequences moderated a lot of my actions.

And so, life was carefree, and I was able to explore my new world for the period from age ten to sixteen without many constraints being placed upon me and my focus was on doing everything that I could in the least amount of time I could. Mam and Ted provided food and shelter and a modicum of direction, mostly in the form of retribution for my indiscretions, but apart from this they were simply people who lived in the same house.

CHAPTER FIVE

SCARY MOMENTS

You have no doubt guessed by now that I was, and still am, a football fanatic. Kicking footballs and any other object was part of my daily routine. Cans, old apples, bits of wood and rocks were all fair game and would be seen flying through the air to announce my arrival. It was the latter that provided one of those scary moments. New Maltkiln Cottages had been built with some cut and fill requirement, that meant the approach to our side gate was about four feet higher than the house itself. As I approached this gate there loomed before me a wonderfully shaped rock that spoke to me and said, "Please kick me." My brain saw only a football and the opportunity to score the winning goal for Newcastle to lift the FA Cup Trophy yet again, and so I kicked it with my best shot. Now the rock sped housebound at approximately four feet from the ground and I suddenly realised what I had done, but to be fair it only made a small bullet-like hole in the frosted window of the bathroom and at this point I briefly believed that the damage might not be immediately obvious. The blood-curdling scream that followed made me reassess this scenario. How could I have known that Ted would be attending to his daily routine at this precise moment in time, and how was I to know that this missile that I had launched would pass perilously close to his head? For these things I could have possibly escaped with no more than a clip under the ear and a tongue lashing. It was the fact that he was in the process of shaving that made all the difference. Ted was "old-fashioned" in a lot of ways and the use of safety razors had not yet appealed to him, and so he used a cutthroat razor to remove those unsightly whiskers and the full meaning of "cutthroat" was about to become very obvious to me. After the scream I had decided to hoof it away from there and just before I rounded the end of the malt kiln, I chanced a look behind and wished immediately that I hadn't. Ted was just emerging from behind the coalhouse brandishing the razor as his singlet turned red and his face was covered in red foam, and I thought for sure that he was going to die soon after he had killed me, and so I made the decision that I would not return home for at least a few years. I did return however after a few days and tried to sneak in after dark and go straight to my bed, which probably made matters worse because I copped an almighty flogging for my original sin and extra for not staying to face the music. Ted was covered in plasters and I don't think staying would have made it any easier.

One of my regular tasks was to "get the coke in". For those of you who have now formed some opinion that I was entangled with a drug-crazed family using their children to obtain the object of their addiction, I will explain what "getting the coke in" meant. Evidently if you process anthracite coal in a certain way there is a by-product which resembles chunks of grey Crunchie bar, and this product is cheaper than coal but burns very efficiently, and at a more even temperature, especially as a fuel for furnaces such as were used to dry grain in the malt kiln. As a perk of being employed by the company, Ted was allowed to use the coke to burn in the slow combustion stove in the cottage, and it was my job to get two buckets each day and put them in the coalhouse for Mam to use. The stove provided the heat, hot water, cooking, and clothes-drying for the household, and as mentioned earlier this was a very efficient design as long as the stove was kept going. And so, at the end of each day, off I went to get the coke in. ·

There were two routes that I could take to achieve this which were simply outside or inside of the malt kiln. During the summer months of course outside was the best option because of the long daylight hours and warm balmy evenings but in the cold, dark, snowy, wet and wintry evenings it was warmer to go through the malt kiln. I should point out that there were some things that I had learned about my mam at this point and one of them was that she saw, felt, and heard things that other people couldn't, and she revelled in telling anyone who would listen of the wondrous things she had experienced. I think that perhaps the daily routine stuff about peoples' relationships become so routine that they simply blend in, and as such become highly forgettable, whilst this sort of spooky stuff remains vivid forever. She told me stories of people who hanged themselves off the steps leading down to the drying floor and that she could feel a tightness in her throat if she passed there. And she talked of the moans and cries from the labourers in the various parts of the building and saw the ghostly figures pleading with her for assistance. In general, I thought she was just trying to scare me half to death, however later in life I believed she was afflicted, and I think there is even a name for it.

Anyway, as you can now understand getting the coke in winter was at best scary. So please pick up your two buckets and let us go through the malt kiln one snowy and windswept winter's night and we can share the nightmare that I endured. Don't worry, for all of the years that I did this I didn't actually see or hear anything... I think! The first part was easy as I collected the buckets from the coal house and walked the thirty or so yards to the entry gantry and up the first four steps and across the wooden loading deck to the top of the stairs leading down to the drying floor. A wooden door with a metal latch opened up to the top of these stairs which were extremely steep, in fact almost like a ladder. There were no lights in this section and so the descent was by feel, whilst all the time waiting for the hand to grasp my scrawny legs and send me cartwheeling to my doom. Each step moaned and groaned under even my paltry weight, and I was sure that I too could feel the tightening of the rope around my neck. And then I was at the bottom and feeling my way along the wall for the door into the drying room, all the while expecting a ghostly hand to reach out for me and whisk me away to some unknown hell. Find the doorway and turn right and follow that wall until at last there is a light switch. After I turned the light on you would think that my dread would be relieved. The drying room is about the size of a small football pitch and there are a series of light switches along the wall. At one end is a water bath which stretches fully across the building and about four feet deep and wide. From this are a series of overhead rails with buckets like cauldrons suspended from them to distribute the wet grain across all of the drying room floor, with the floor above held up by many pillars that now cast ghostly shadows everywhere. As I progressed along the wall treading in about six inches of wet barley and turning lights on as I went, I realised that I was sweating and waiting for that life-ending event to happen. Some tormented figure that would emerge from within the shadows to tear you from limb to limb or that sudden attack from behind that makes you turn around frequently only to quickly look back. It's a wonder that I didn't end up with a neck like a bird with all around vision. Finally, I'm in the furnace room stumbling on bits of broken coke as I search for yet another light switch to illuminate the mountain of coke from which I quickly fill my buckets. This part of the journey is the most relaxing because it is now totally light with the lights and the glow from the furnaces and it is pleasantly warm. I take the opportunity to read the graphs of the kiln temperatures to report back to Ted if there is a large variation. Then it's lights out and the return journey. Returning and turning lights out only heightens the feeling that some evil is waiting to pounce on you from behind and the climb back up the stairs still makes me feel that someone or something is going to grasp my leg through the steps and plunge me to my doom. Finally, I'm back on the gantry and my arms feel as if they will fall off but I won't stop until I'm back in the cold wintry night and the buckets are safely in the coal room.

The elation that I felt at this point was almost intoxicating and made me feel exceptionally alive. There were some nights, as you may understand, when I simply did not get the coke in and gladly accepted the repercussions when I got home knowing that Ted had to get two buckets in during the day. I have ridden horses in unpassable country, camped in Yeti country, and experienced life in Vietnam, and nothing as yet compares with "getting the coke in".

At some point during my time at Thirsk my stepbrother David and I must have developed something close to a mutual understanding of our roles in the household, and as such he became far more tolerant of me and my presence to the point where he accepted me hanging around when he was doing important stuff like working on his car. He had an old Ford with running boards and shiny chrome spoked wheels and leather upholstery which smelled like the Humber Snipe that was the car at Ramle. It was the most beautiful car that I have ever seen with chrome diamond-shaped wheel nuts and chrome door handles, and I pictured myself as a gangster driving the streets with my gunnies on the running boards as I terrorised the local populace. I was like a moth drawn to a murderous light every time I saw this highly polished black car and was transfixed each time I was allowed to sit in the driver's seat, and touch things that I thought made me like Sterling Moss winning racing accolades at Brands Hatch with Fangio left in my wake. Can you imagine then the feeling of exultation when one day he said, "Would you like to back it out?" He was going to let me drive his car: but wait, this was probably a way for him to tease me by waiting until I got excited then refusing me the pleasure and then laughing like some hyena at the kill. But no, he was seriously going to let me drive his car and jumped in beside me on the passenger side. "Turn this key and push that black button," he said, and the engine burst into life as he slapped my finger off the black button to save his starter motor from burning out. My legs and arms turned to jelly and I'm sure that I felt faint, and the pit of my stomach warned me of the terrible things that were going to happen shortly, but I wanted to drive so, so badly. "Now, don't touch that one, push this one in and release it slowly when I tell you", were instructions that I have since given and with the same effect. I pushed this one in and David jiggled a lever that I have since come to know as the gearstick, and he instructed me to slowly release it. I should have told him that my legs where incapable of any controlled movement and that we should terminate the exercise here and now, but damn it I was Sterling Moss and had a race to win. At about this time "this one" developed a mind of its own and decided to fully release somewhat more quickly than was required, causing the car to lurch and jump backwards quite fiercely and out of its garaged area and into the twenty yards between the gantry and the house. With any luck it would have stalled and come to a halt with only a substantial amount of yelling and cursing, but no such luck for this was a strong-willed vehicle of substantial construction. At a sedate but constant speed it crossed the twenty yards quite comfortably and to his credit David had regained his composure and instructed me to push "this thing" fully in. Most boys of my age would have done the same thing that I did next and that was to miss "this thing" and push "that one" which caused this sedate reversing to become accelerated carnage on wheels. I still believe that it was the embankment which caused the sudden momentum to give us sufficient speed to crash through the fence and into Ted's vegetable garden rather than any fault of the driver, which is a term that could be loosely applied to me. At this point I had my first piece of good fortune in as much as Ted had just finished preparation of the vegetable beds, which caused the car to become hopelessly bogged to the running boards and stall. At the same time, I did what any boy with self-preservation on his mind would do and bolted while David tried desperately to get his door open against one of Ted's potato mounds. Not having to jump the fence gave me the edge and in a flash I was gone and hiding in the malt kiln where I just happened to know where Ted's binoculars where hiding. The last that I saw was Penty's tractor pulling the car out of the garden and everyone pointing at various things and looking fairly agitated.

I can never remember David being so lenient as he was after this incident. No kicking or punching or verbal abuse. He just looked empty and forlorn: after all it was only a car.

CHAPTER SIX

MY SPORTING PROWESS

I'm fourteen and turned out in my whites for the Junction Cricket Team. I probably look like some skinny white stork but in my head I'm all the greatest cricketers ever to grace the Oval or Headingly. In my mind I've won this game a hundred times with that diving catch at first slip, the ball that moves off the seam to dismiss the star batsmen and not to forget that direct hit that runs out their big hitter.

Whilst none of these eventuated, I did bowl and field well but will be remembered for forgetting to wear a protector, or as we called them a "box", when batting. Even at fourteen I was aware of the need to protect "them" for future use but simply forgot in my rush to go out and bat. I have never been much with the bat but could stick around a bit and hold an end up; they often refer to batsmen like me as "ferrets" because we went in after the bunnies. But this was my first innings for the men's team and I was really keen to impress. The pads that I wore felt like they were made for a giant and they slapped me on the thighs with every step and the bat felt like it weighed a ton with gloves still sweaty from the previous batsman, and then I realised that I didn't have my box on. Too late, I told myself, and honestly didn't think it would be necessary and there was probably only the one that the last batsman had, which was not a good thought.

And so, I strode to the crease and asked for middle and leg

from the umpire and was soon to add a new meaning to this guard. The first delivery was a wicked delivery at about four hundred miles per hour which jagged back off a good length, the type of ball that would have beaten Dexter let alone this skinny fourteen-year-old. There are two things that allowed me to escape the LBW appeal; one was that it was too high and the other was that no one could stop laughing long enough to appeal. Yes, all of you males will know that the pain is excruciating but those around you have to laugh. It's not that they hate you but rather that they are thankful it's not them. "Are you OK?", and "Poor kid, hasn't used them yet", and "Shall we book you into the monastery lad?" all seem to be said in jest as they winced.

And who is going to administer first aid I ask you? Indeed, who at fourteen is going to expose the battered items to a group of tittering adults, who seem to find it all hilarious. So you roll around for a while and wipe the tears from your eyes and squeak, "I'm all right, honest." Afterwards you inspect the damaged parts thoroughly and wonder if it has any long-term effect. My four children may take a moment to reflect on this in hindsight.

Did we win the game? No. Did I score any runs? No. And did I remember the match? Yes. Apart from the injury I bowled well and took three for twenty-seven off nine overs on a beautiful summer evening at Kilburn on the hills at the edge of the Yorkshire moors.

These cricketing days were some of the most wonderful days because we played in all the villages in the region and it is one of the most beautiful areas in all of England and the cricket grounds were simply breathtaking. But most of all, after the game was over, we would all get on the bus and head to the nearest pub. Of course Tich and I could never go into the bar but the men brought us shandies and packets of potato crisps and chocolate bars. And we would sit back in the lounge area and play darts and pretend we were so grown up.

Cricket has been the sport to cause me more pain and injury than any other. In all the years that I have played football the worst that has occurred is some grazing on the legs from slide tackling. Even a stint at school hockey pales when compared to cricket.

As with all sports we practised as keenly as we played in cricket and these practice sessions could be like war zones if you weren't on your mettle. Everyone would bowl and bat and there where literally dozens of balls going in every different direction. As you got a ball you bowled at one of the batsmen and then retrieved your ball or some players would roam the boundary and throw the balls back to the stumps. Batsmen unsure of who was bowling, bowlers unsure of who was bowling, balls being returned from the boundary and general chaos was the scene for tragedy. In later life I have been trained in matters of occupational health and safety and when we say that the situation is already an accident just waiting for the consequence this could well have been a training aid to prove the theory. I heard the shout of "look out" but on that field of chaos I was totally unaware of from where or in what form the "look out" was coming from. The natural reaction was to turn and see what was happening, and in retrospect it was probably fortunate as the ball hit me on the side of the nose instead of the back of the head. It was a return from the boundary that was almost perfectly over the stumps and the pain was pretty bad, but luckily short lived as I only remember waking up at home to find breathing and looking to be almost impossible. Everyone said I was lucky to only have a broken nose and some lacerations from my broken glasses, but if this was being lucky then I'm glad I wasn't unlucky. I forgot to mention that whilst in Ramle it was discovered that I was short sighted and after testing my eyes I was given a pair of wire-rimmed spectacles that looked much like the ones that Harry Potter has, only mine never seemed to be clean and rarely sat straight on my head. I was to get broad-rimmed ones later and everyone said I looked like Buddy Holly, which I took as a compliment.

The ensuing events highlight my relationship with mater and step pater when I needed to go to York to have my nose set. Instead of parental support I was given the bus fare and told, "Off you go." I could barely see the bus let alone the destination window, and when I finally got to York if it weren't for the kindly locals, I could have been there for days trying to find the hospital. Anyone who has had their nose reset can attest to the pain involved and that I found my way home again after that was a miracle. The saving grace in all of this was that I didn't get a clip under the ear for breaking my spectacles and the new pair were a lot trendier.

Much later in life someone invented indoor cricket which I love as it is a fast and furious indoor sport like indoor soccer. However, even in this form of the game I managed a major injury, which I shall relate later.

After a short time in Thirsk, I learned to ride a bicycle, which I hadn't had the opportunity to do in Newcastle. I borrowed one from one of the local lads who was conspicuous by his size or lack of it. "Fish" Hardy was short but that was a bonus for me because I could always put my feet down while learning to ride on his machine. I had soon mastered the art and rode everywhere, as was the case for every child that I knew. The problem was that the borrowed machine was now too small for me so imagine my delight when I got the paper boy job which came with an extremely large red bike with panniers and mechanical brakes and wheels the size of those on a small motorbike.

You may well ask what this has to do with sporting prowess and that would be a fair question. Something which was developed into a sporting achievement was the ability to dink as many people as possible on a bike along the length of the narrow cinder path leading to Railway Terrace. Many had achieved three people and some had attempted four but no one had ever attempted six. It was a record that beckoned our group of idiots and one that we had to achieve.

The paper boy bike was the ideal vehicle to attempt the record on because of the frame over the back wheel and the two paper panniers on the frame. And so, we practiced with one in each pannier, one on the frame, one on the seat, me pedalling, and one on the handlebars. Time after time we tried to become mobile, and time after time, we ended up a tangled web of legs, arms and bicycle. But we were undeterred and I had convinced everyone that if we could actually get some forward momentum then we could achieve the cinder path course. All of you who have attempted something like this would know that the most difficult part was always gaining that forward momentum to enable you to keep the whole thing balanced. We finally worked out that if the two inside the panniers were to stand and lean forward it gave me enough chance by starting with the pedal at its highest point to get moving. The first fifty yards was slightly downhill and then a gradual uphill run for the remaining hundred yards if we were to make it from gate to gate as the record required. On the appointed day, the intrepid six mounted and after a couple of false starts we were off and pedalling down the first fifty yards. I should point out that the cinder track was bordered on both sides by a wooden fence and the cinders were crushed residue from the kiln furnaces which had been rolled down with a heavy roller to provide a surface for the railway workers to walk to work.

That first fifty yards was achieved without incident except that Baz Foster and Fish Hardy began to get tired of their standing positions and their shuffling made balancing more difficult. We had reached what would nowadays be termed optimum forward momentum as we started the slight uphill section, and with some shouted instruction to Baz and Fish I started to grow in confidence. Pedalling was becoming more and more difficult, and I started to feel the pain in my legs, and at that point realised the futility of our attempt but could not tell the others for fear of inducing panic in my passengers. I don't think anyone would have done any better than we did in that attempted world record, nor would the end result have been more full of carnage, than that which we achieved.

Still well short of our objective I developed what is termed the death wobbles and the handlebars clipped the wooden fence, bringing the attempt to a sudden and disastrous end. Luckily, there was no requirement for hospitalisation for any of the daredevils, however Mrs Foster, Baz's mother, took quite some time to stem all of the blood flows and remove the pieces of crushed cinder from various body locations, and she used gallons of purple stuff which, although it stung terribly, I at least refrained from crying. She had no sticky tape left nor any cotton wool and she constantly kept saying things like, "You should have known better Robin Hepple" and "Whatever possessed you to do such a silly thing?" Little did she appreciate that had we achieved the record we would have become instant heroes in the Junction. I might point out here that the paper bike was unharmed, and we did manage the cinder path with four on it to become the only ones to achieve that number.

I was never very good at athletics, although cross country running, along with most distance running, always made me feel alive and as such, I would enter all of these events. The really good thing about cross country running was that I by now knew almost every field and track and all of the woodland areas in the district, and for some reason the runs always started and finished at the school football grounds and as such it made it very easy to make some tactical changes to the marked route. The problem with this was that by finishing in the top group of runners you could get nominated for competitions away from the areas that were well known. The other problem was that when you re-joined the run you ran the risk of some really good runner spotting you and referring it to some teacher or in particular to Mr Rawlins the PE teacher. Mr Rawlins had a soft spot for me for two reasons: I was the junior football captain, and I delivered his newspaper each morning and told no one of the magazines to which he subscribed. He could not turn a blind eye to outright cheating however, and when required would mete out the most common punishment involving a cane and a private part of my anatomy, which was covered at all times. I found out later that I could outlast the majority of children and didn't need to take shortcuts at all. It was never as much fun though.

Football was the reason that I existed and during the season I rarely spent a day without in some way playing or practising to play the game. By the time I was fourteen I was the Junior House Captain of Peregrine at Thirsk school, captain of the school junior football team, had played for the North Riding and turned out every week for the local men's team. I dreamed of playing at senior level with Newcastle United, Middlesbrough, or even York or Hartlepool, and wanted at that stage to go to university and become a Physical Education teacher to enhance my chances of fulfilling my football dream. Every time I ran onto a football field, I was full of nervous tension and then after the kick-off it would disappear and be replaced with feelings of elation and anticipation. It is difficult for me to explain because I am not very articulate, but the feelings that I had when playing football were so intense that they became physical and I had never felt the same way about anything else in my life right up until I left England and travelled to Australia.

Playing for the Junction team was the most daunting for me because it was against grown men, whereas in school football I was normally one of the bigger participants. Tich and I were the only "lads" to play and we always played in the forwards because it was safer for us there. We both played our hearts out and were rewarded by scoring goals that in our school football was a rarity, both being defenders. In retrospect we were well protected by the other players and any heavy tackles usually brought some form of protest from our team. No particular game or event sticks in the memory more than any other because every game was so special and those feelings were with me every time I played.

CHAPTER SEVEN

IT'S TIME TO EARN YOUR KEEP

Almost to the day of my thirteenth birthday Ted decided that I should start to contribute to my keep and as such he got me a job as a Paper Boy with the lady who ran the news stand on the railway station. Her name was Mrs Thatcher and I often wondered since if she was related to the first female British Prime Minister. She was a matronly lady and I mean no pun when I say that but she could have been Mrs Tait's sister and was just as bossy and fussy. I later found out that she and Ted had planned this for some time and had only waited until now because thirteen was the legal age for a youth to take on employment of this nature. As you know the job came with a big red paper bike which I was allowed to keep for the period of time that I was the paper boy and that was for two and a half years.

I had no say in the matter and could not hide the fact that I was paid ten shillings a week because it was all pre-arranged and my contribution to the household was the whole ten shillings. The idea was that Mam would use the money to buy my clothes and school requirements but this never worked out because she had no idea of what clothes a teenager wanted. She preferred sturdy shoes and trousers with cuffs that made your legs look like broomsticks in grain sacks and things with no colour in them. We came to an agreement that I could keep half of my ten shillings and buy my own clothes which would include brightly colour pinstripe drainpipe jeans and winkle picker shoes and a jacket with no lapel when the Beatles became the in group. I have never been and probably never will be trendy but at least I now had the chance to look reasonably good on the rare times that I got to go to the pictures or parties.

The paper round also gave me the opportunity to develop some social skills which up until now I had totally lacked. The people of the round got to know me and I was well-respected by them for the manner in which I carried out those tasks. I always made sure that the papers and magazines were in the best possible condition when the customers got them even if it meant separating them before sliding them into the door slots. In those days, and I presume still today, houses had spring loaded flaps in their doors to allow papers and mail to be transferred straight into them. Some people actually put the house key on a piece of string inside the flap and I could never understand this, you might as well leave the door unlocked. Anyway, my upbringing ensured that I had enough self-discipline to do the job to the very best of my ability.

Every morning at five o'clock I would get up and by half past would be on the railway station to load up the papers. The weather conditions were totally irrelevant in this equation and Mrs Thatcher would give me what for if I was late and I don't know what she would have done if I didn't turn up at all. Ted would probably not have been very appreciative either. These things were not the driving factors however—it was that I really wanted to do the round every day. Once at the station I would load the papers into the paniers in the correct order of delivery, get any special instructions and off I would go. The first couple of weeks were difficult because I was unsure of the names of all the customers, but Mrs Thatcher wrote on each delivery until I was confident. During that first period my biggest dread was losing control of the bike and having papers strewn all over the place. This did happen a couple of times later on but by then I simply put them back in the correct sequence and carried on with the round.

Even today I could probably do that same round again. From the station it was off to the Cree's who had the local taxi and I was mates with their son Paul, then across to the Old Red House pub run by the Beadles who had two daughters, Geraldine and Angela. From there over the railway bridge to the Ritchies who owned the potato processing factory. The Ritchies had four daughters who were mostly older than me and went to posh schools somewhere. Then double back a short way to the Clark's and then down the cinder path to the Railway Cottages. I loved these rows of houses because I could do so many in a short time. And so the round went on to bungalows and terraced houses all with their own strange magazines. My English master had all sorts of literature periodicals and I wondered if I read them would I get the exams in advance but could never get the time to stop. And a chap who lived by himself near Tin Tack Lane got magazines of body builders and weightlifting but he was a small weedy looking fellow. Dinger Bell got fishing magazines and Mr Rawlins, well I can't say, but I would often sneak a peek at his.

On Saturday morning it was money collection day and most of the people would leave their money out for me whilst some preferred me to knock and wait. I would collect and deliver on my way through the round and collect again on the way back. Each time I got money I had to cross it off in a book and show the customer if they were there. To do this I carried a leather pouch much the same as the clippys on the buses and at the end of the round I took the book and the money pouch back to Mrs

Thatcher to count it. During my time as a paper boy, I can never remember any customer having problems with their money. Perhaps honesty was not an issue in rural Yorkshire in the early sixties or perhaps my memory doesn't want to remember the negatives. If the money was correct then I was finished for the day and got my ten shillings payment, if the money was up it went into a jar, and if it was down, we made it up from the jar, or it was deducted from my wages. I didn't see this as being unfair, it simply made me more diligent with handling money.

Christmas time, or should I say just prior to Christmas, was the most satisfying time for paper boys. I would take a separate bag with me on collection days and made heaps in tips from my satisfied customers, which was all of them. Chris Beadle at the pub always gave me ten shillings which was great at the start of the round. I made sure that I called on everybody in the couple of weeks leading up to Christmas and all of the tips went into my pocket. In truth I did give Mam some so that they wouldn't enquire too much on how much I made. And so, I kept the paper boy job up until just before I left England, and Ted even used to congratulate me on the comments he got from people in the Junction and he would say, "We'll make somat of thee yet lad." Too late Ted, my departure was imminent.

I did have other jobs in the last few months before leaving England and mostly to get enough money together for the journey without letting Ted or Mam know the true reason for my mad saving spree. The paper bike was also a fine vehicle to cart an extension ladder and bucket with cloths in. I pedalled everywhere and cleaned windows for people on the paper route and anyone that they recommended me to. This was a good earner but it was also extremely hard work. When I gave up the paper round, I spent some time sorting potatoes at the factory that the Ritchies had, and then was a truck driver's offsider to deliver bags of spuds all over northeast England. I was on the road for days and the driver only drove the truck, while I had to load and unload the potatoes. If he left at four in the morning then I had to load the truck and tarp it down the previous afternoon and at each stop such as the Smiths Crisp factories I had to unload the correct number of sacks. All of this was done with a sack barrow and no such things as pallets and forklifts for me. The truck was an AEC Mercury, and the passenger seat couldn't be secured because the battery was under it, and so every time we went around a corner I had to hang on for dear life, especially in the summer when the window was down because the seat was as high as the window. But it was better than sorting spuds which was done on a conveyor after they had been through a wash which made the work dirty, wet, and back-breaking.

Potatoes were a major source of income in my district and each year we would get work at one of the farms taity scratting (potato picking). With a basket we would follow the turned over rows and pick up the potatoes. When your basket was full then you tipped it in a trailer that was pulled along behind an old Fergie tractor. It always amazed me because no one actually drove the tractor until the trailer was full and then it was taken to be buried in a "pie" until sold at a later date. The work was back-breaking and we school kids were not paid for volume but on an hourly rate which was hardly enough to buy our smokes let alone anything useful.

Although I always seemed to have some money, I worked hard for it and always gave Mam some of it for my keep. I resented parting with my hard-earned cash but did learn that I respected the fact that it cost money to feed and look after me and took that lesson with me into my adulthood.

There was one other benefit in earning a little bit of money and that was it gave me the options of other forms of entertainment, some of which I now regret immensely. By the time I was fifteen, I was often running errands for Ted to get his Woodbines, and whilst earlier I would manage one from his pack at home, I could now buy my own pack of five smokes. In all honesty not all of them were for my own consumption but rather they were a means of getting lots of other things and favours. There was an acceptance of smoking in those days and even movie stars smoked on screen as a sort of "macho" thing. Cigarette advertising was big business and sporting events relied on the tobacco companies for their pounds. There was one particularly obnoxious cigarette called Ardath which had a loose cork filter that tasted awful but had a catchy jingle:

Ardath, Ardath you're a star

Beat the other smokes by far.

Sung to the "Twinkle, Twinkle Little Star" tune.

I even got to know what the "Durex" sign in tiny writing in Hardy's shop window was all about.

Earning my own money got me the necessary clothing to be "cool" and get invited to parties. Most of which were simply spin the bottle, balloons and cake dos but the one at the Air Cadets was something else. "Party" is only a loose term and it started out much the same with all the boys sitting around the outside of the hall and the girls dancing with each other. Then suddenly all the lights went out and the girls rushed over to sit on a boy's knee but not knowing which one. There was much snogging and this went on all night until we all went off to our homes with the girls all giggling and the boys lying about touching this one up and stuff. Really harmless fun, but we thought we were just it. This party was enough prompting for me to join the Air Cadets.

We met every week and learned morse code, how to recognise aeroplanes from their silhouettes, and how to talk on the military radios. The uniforms were RAF surplus from the war days and the battle dress was too large and felt like I was clothed in a hessian bag. It must have been hilarious to watch me peddling on the paper bike with my skinny little arms and head protruding from this blue prickly cover as if I was the victim of head shrinking natives. Worse was the chaffing on the inside of the legs which made me walk like I was too many years as The Cisco Kid's offsider. The climax was when I was one of the lucky ones to go to Southampton Air Base for a week with the real airmen. We lived in the barracks, got yelled at a lot, ate their shitty food, and were told everything to do. I loved it. It was just like Butlins revisited. And the climax of the climax was the day we went up, yes up there, in the sky. I don't remember the name of the plane but seem to recollect something like a Hercules, and as we trooped on, we were given a small brown paper bag, but I was confused because it never had any lunch or a piece of fruit in it, just an empty paper bag. We were told to use the bag and not the floor, strange people these Raffles. Seat belts checked, we taxied to our runway with this plane feeling like a giant mixmaster, all shaking and noise. We were then informed that we would be doing "Circuits and Bumps" and the plane leaped forward and got noisier until a sudden quiet, and I've got the feeling that I'm laying down and the front of the plane is thirty feet above me and the seat is trying to eat me. Then we levelled off and banked heavily to one side so that I was looking directly at the ground and my seat belt was now trying to devour me. More banking, and then we descended back towards the runway, and I was feeling a little queasy but had seen others use the paper bag and now knew its use. My stomach was somewhere on the roof of the plane by now and I desperately needed to pee and was thankful that it was all over as the tyres screeched on the tarmac. But we didn't slow down, in fact we accelerated again and once again I was looking at the cabin thirty feet above me and there was a chain reaction of paper bags. We did two more "Circuits and Bumps" before we were allowed to feel terra firma again and we each carried a full "lunch bag" to the latrines—military talk for toilets—and my Air Force career was over and I wished that I hadn't been one of the lucky ones to be able to afford the trip. The Air Cadet adventure was to serve me well later because I had shown some interest in the RAF.

CHAPTER EIGHT

MY BIGGEST DECISION

After four years of my life in Thirsk I was again resigned to the fact that this was how I would live my life. It was mapped out and I was happy enough to finish Grammar School and move on to university and subsequent stardom on the football field. I had the freedom to come and go as I liked, was part of the community, had lots of friends, and as long as I did the few domestic chores required of me, I was pretty well left alone. There were no attendances by either parent at any event that I participated in, either sport or school, and I neither expected nor got any semblance of acceptance as part of the family group except for the occasion when I was told that I was being adopted into Ted's family which changed my name from Hepple to Reed. It was all done in absentia and I wasn't consulted in the matter. Just that one day I'm Robin Clive Hepple and the next I'm Robin Clive Reed. No big ceremony or little party or hugs and playful banter, just Hepple then Reed. I often thought of changing it back, but in reality, I didn't think that I owed anything to my birth name either. I was tolerated rather than included but had now gained wide acceptance in my outside world.

At some stage we went to Kirkaldy in Scotland to visit with one of Ted's sisters and it was quite boring because I was taken away from my friends and my life and made to enter theirs. During the visit I heard lots of talk about someone called James who was evidently Ted's nephew because they called him my cousin and he'd gone to Australia and was a big shot in some airline company over there. I was again given the freedom to wander the town and did so at each opportunity but there were no open spaces and I was only a wee sassenach, something of a side show rather than a visitor. They'd say to Ted, "Is that Dot's boy" and he'd reply, "Yeh" and that was it, once again it was a tolerance thing not a "Come in and have a wee bit cake laddie" thing.

The reason that I mention this visit however is to introduce you to Cousin James who had gone off to Australia and joined QANTAS in their freight department and had indeed risen to be a big shot—he was a supervisor at a freight building in Sydney. He becomes the most important person in my life for about twelve months although I was to only meet him three times. Late in the summer of my fifteenth year, cousin James visited his Uncle Ted at Maltkiln Cottages and arrived in a flash hire car with a tan like some West Indian cricketer. For some reason he took a shine to me and spent lots of time talking to me about Australia. Sunshine, bikini clad girls on golden beaches, beer flowing from every tap, and work wherever you went. A land of opportunity he told me, and they speak English too. OK I was a naïve young lad who believed everything he said and could almost taste the good life of which he spoke. I started to read everything I could about Australia including the colourful brochures that he brought with him, probably from the Qantas advertisements. The more he spoke and the more I read the more I wanted to go there.

James had given me a mountain of information including some literature from a group called The Big Brother Movement who sponsored boys from England and found them employment in Australia. It only cost sixteen quid and this was refunded to you when you went to your first job. A "Big Brother" escorted these "Little Brothers" on the journey and there was a lovely little dairy to help your adjustment to the Australian way when you got there waiting for the job that they found. I suspect that the jobs where all prearranged with certain employers who could use some cheap labour. But it sounded like the place for me. I have since found out that James worked in Hunter Street in Sydney, which is also the street that the Big Brother Movement are housed in, and I wonder if there was some connection.

Full of enthusiasm, I blurted out my intention to Mam and Ted as soon as James had once more returned to his land of milk and honey. I should point out at this time that James, for some reason, returned to Scotland and went to work in a mine within a couple of years of this rhetoric of a promised land. For me it was too late. Imagine my total shock when I was fairly bluntly told, "No! Tha's not goin'. Tha'll do the school and then go ta the university." This was Ted, the most he had said to me in four years was his Yorkshire greeting of "Now then" or "I'll teach yer to do that" or "It'll make a man of yer." And here he was denying me the chance to further my life in Australia. They hadn't shown this much raw emotion in four years and now they chose to say no. "I divnt gi a bugger," said I, "I'm awa." I pleaded, they refused and threatened my very life. I yelled and they yelled, I got more clouts and eventually we reached a compromise. I could apply to join the RAF because my stepbrother Michael had been in the RAF and it made a man of him. And so, I acquired all of the papers for the RAF and all of the papers for the Big Brother Movement and filled them all in, and as Ted was leaving for his Buffs meeting, I thrust them under his glass eye and asked for his signature where indicated. As I had guessed the Buffs were too important to waste time scanning through all this paperwork, and he could see RAF on the top sheet and so he signed all the paperwork as requested.

Of course the RAF paperwork went in the bin and I watched every mail delivery for weeks until a manila envelope arrived with the details of my emigration to Australia. "I've been accepted for the RAF and have to be in Southampton on a given day in April to do an apprenticeship as an Aircraft Fitter" I lied. "Well done lad," Ted offered, "It'll make a man of yer." And so, on the given day I caught the train from Thirsk to London, and then under the supervision of my "Big Brother" on to Harwich and the MS Aurelia bound for Sydney, Australia.

I had promised to write when I got there and so I did some weeks later:

Dear Mam and Ted,

Sorry to have taken so long to write but the voyage was quite rough and I'm not a good sailor. We arrived safely in Australia and I'm working on a property called Lanyon Station and you can't imagine the size of the place.

Anyway I've got to run now as I'm due back at work.

All the best,
Robin

I think that at about the time of receiving this note they started to show some real emotion.

CHAPTER NINE

LIFE ON THE HIGH SEAS

The MS Aurelia had the same sort of life history as I had and has been passed from one situation to another throughout her life. She was given life in 1939 in Hamburg at the same time as the Bismark was being built, and under the name of MS Huascaran she served as a submarine depot and supply ship for the German Navy, and after the war she was placed on the coast of South America service. Perhaps she took some of the war criminals to South America. In 1947, the year of my birth, she was sold to Canadian Pacific, renamed Beaverbrae, and used to repatriate displaced persons to Germany, and later to carry emigrants to Canada. In 1954, she was sold to the Codegar Line in Genoa, Italy, refitted and renamed the MS Aurelia to be operated on the New Zealand and Australia run.

And so, at Harwich I boarded her under the supervision of my "Big Brother" and along with fifteen or so other boys for our journey to Sydney, Australia. Aurelia was approximately ten thousand tons and although small in comparison with others it was huge to me. We boys were housed in two cabins with bunk style sleeping for eight in each cabin, whilst our big brother was somewhere else on the ship, and he wouldn't tell us where. The daily routine started with physical training including calisthenics and a run around the ship, then the day was basically ours to do as we wished. For all but me this routine started on day one but I didn't do anything until day five. It was at this time that I realised that I suffer badly from motion sickness to the point where I was bedridden for those first days. I had heard people say that they would have gladly died rather than feel as sick as you get with seasickness and I know that this is true. After four days of regurgitating everything that passed my lips, I had become seriously dehydrated, and whilst skinny to start I was now malnourished. The bedside light had shorted and given me an electric shock, and I would have thrown myself overboard if I could have stayed upright long enough to reach even the lowest of decks.

Someone must have realised that I could not continue like this or else they would have to perform a burial at sea on a passenger liner. So I was taken to the sickbay on a stretcher and an Italian doctor, who must have been a sadist, advised that I would have to have an injection. I don't know what the substance was but it was administered through a needle in my backside that could easily have passed through both cheeks and definitely changed my mind about death from seasickness to death from stab wounds to the buttocks. The doctor then left instructions to administer another needle at some later date if I didn't make a recovery. Whether it was the threat of another needle or the substance working I don't know, but I made a miraculous recovery and suffered no more seasickness on the voyage.

And so, I missed the first part of the journey, and not until we hit the Mediterranean, did I feel the balmy sea breeze blowing in my face whilst doing the morning exercises with big brother. With plimsolls, shorts, and white tee shirt, we would prance around like naval cadets near the pool and then off around the ship, going up and down gangways with mad abandon until we realised that once again our big brother was nowhere to be seen, and we went back to our cabins.

Meals were served in sittings and most of the time we had no idea what it was that we were eating other than it was Italian. Even the English meals were Italian but at least we were introduced to the habit of drinking red wine with meals, as part of the digestive system we were told. Sixteen-year-olds have not got any ability to consume wine at dinner and consequently I would end up sloshed after a couple of glasses, however I still enjoy a red with a good spag bol. The food in general was ordinary but we developed a good rapport with our waiter, and he helped out as much as he could with interpretations, and probably got a fair amount of red wine left after dinner to satisfy his own needs. Days were spent playing cards, reading, and generally exploring around the ship and at the duty-free shop, where cigarettes and spirits were dirt cheap and kept us anaesthetised constantly.

After sailing through the calm of the Mediterranean we stopped at Port Said on the northern end of the Suez Canal joining the Mediterranean and Red Seas. Although we didn't disembark there, we got the opportunity to do shopping for the luxuries available on the many small boats that surrounded the ship. The traders would display their wares to the passengers and there would be much bartering when the passengers would offer what they thought were ridiculous offers only to have a counter bid launched back at them. I imagine it was like a floating bazaar with total distrust by the passengers and a worldly knowledge from the traders and noise that made understanding almost impossible. It was, of course, too much for me to bear, and I started to bid on this magnificent gold watch, which I was assured was of the finest Swiss movement and the band alone would be worth a fortune. I started ridiculously low as instructed and was greeted with a term that I heard often from the traders, "You think I'm a fool Mr McKenzie?" I have no idea how many Misters McKenzie there were on the ship because everyone was addressed this way.

We finally agreed on thirty shillings, which I believed was an absolute steal, and then we argued for another ten minutes about who was passing what first. "You send up the watch," I called down to him, and he countered "You think I'm a fool Mr McKenzie? You send the money in my basket, and I send the watch." We eventually made the exchange, and I must admit that I sent the money down first and I admired the beautiful watch which shone in the sunlight and felt as though I was the best barterer in the whole world. I realise now of course that these traders have centuries of experience and sixteen-year-old, pimply-faced poms have no idea whatsoever. By the time we reached our next destination of Aden the watch had stopped, never to go again, and became ceremoniously thrown overboard with a curse and in the knowledge that I was an idiot but not alone in that realisation.

The trip through the Canal was absolutely the most unbelievable thing I had witnessed. At times it felt as if we could reach out and grasp handfuls of sand from the desert banks and then we passed through lakes with ships waiting their turn to proceed. There were locals in their robes, some of which were brightly coloured and others plain white, which I learnt was to protect them from the heat as light colours reflect rather than absorb heat. Small villages with green patches of vegetation amongst the seemingly endless sand dotted the banks. And then we are out in the Red Sea and heading south to berth at Aden, where we were allowed off the ship to do some more shopping. I didn't get caught again, but the hustle and bustle, the smells and noise were intoxicating and unlike anything this sixteen-year-old could have ever imagined. I soaked it all in and imagined myself as some Lawrence of Arabia type, gallantly saving the Arab world from oppression and revelling in their gratitude. All very teenagerish I know, but it was so, so good that I couldn't help being overcome by it all. Didn't buy a thing because we were warned off the food and drink although it couldn't have been any worse than that served on board.

Soon we left Aden behind and set across the huge expanse of water that would take us to our first port of call in Australia—Perth. We participated in all of the celebrations on board, including the crossing of the Equator ceremony, which was all too much for me to understand, what with all the mumbo jumbo, and besides I'm sure I had had too many duty-frees on the Lido Deck. And after what seemed like months but was only a couple of weeks, we arrived at Freemantle. My first sighting of my new home, and it is amazing. The sun is like I have never seen before because it is so bright and warm and a gentle warm breeze tugs at my clothing and then flutters off to warm someone else.

Everything seems so fresh and clean and this is only the port. I know immediately that this is the land of plenty and that I'm going to enjoy this place. This feeling is to change often over the next few weeks as I see the huge variation that is the essence of Australia. Those first steps after the crossing of the Indian Ocean made me feel as if I was drunk trying to regain my land legs. There was a group of ladies, quite old ladies, who took us under their wings and showed us the sights of Perth. The first part of the journey was from Freemantle to Perth on a rickety old train, passing behind buildings that resembled what I imagined Dodge City would have looked like. Once again, the thoughts on Australia changed to, "Wow, how old is this place?" At Perth we boarded a bus which took us to the sights of Perth which although I cannot remember them, I do remember changing my mind again as Australia turned into a warm, clean, and beautiful place with lush green parks and modern buildings. How can one small country have so much variation? I was way off the mark again. Back on board, we set off for Melbourne via the Great Australian Bight where I was glad to have got over the seasickness and instead watched others wishing they could pass away and not have to endure the foul feeling.

Melbourne—what can I say. It was late afternoon when we docked in late April in Port Melbourne and it was a dreary sight. We were allowed off the ship and so the group of little brothers caught taxis into Melbourne, and it was after six p.m. in the mid-sixties. Standing outside a Milk Bar wondering what to do and these two rozzers (policemen) brace us up for loitering. PC Dixon would have put us right but these two only want to remove this bunch of delinquent poms back to wherever they came from. I had no idea how the conversation went but we piled back into taxis and went back to the ship and another night of duty-frees. Once again, my assessment of Australia changed, and I was beginning to wonder if this had been the right decision.

On the high seas again this time for the final destination— Sydney. How can one of the major cities in my new homeland be named after Sid Calvert, the snot nosed kid from Thirsk, or any other Sydney for that matter? Anyway, we duly arrived and once again it was late evening, and this time we took all our worldly possessions with us, which for me included a tin of shortbread biscuits and a pair of trousers for Cousin James. Down the gangplank for the last time and this time through customs with a little piece of paper declaring that I carried this Scottish Shortbread lovingly transported from some distant auntie in

Kirkaldy for Cousin James who is now standing waiting to greet me beyond the customs people. No way known am I going to get past these vigilant officers with these lethal biscuits, and James can only watch in horror as they are whisked away, no doubt to be devoured greedily by the customs workers with their evening cuppa. And so here I am standing on Australian terra firma, with no more sailing and adventure on the high seas and shaking hands with James who informs me that his parents have informed him that I was in Southampton with the RAF, and not in a foreign land on the other side of the world. His connection with the Big Brother Movement had however confirmed that I was indeed Australia bound.

My reunion with James was cut short by big brother herding us onto a bus which travelled through the night and eventually pulled up at a "training" farm on Cowpasture Road just outside of Liverpool. We all lugged our kit into this dormitory with beds along either side and were instructed to "Stow your gear and get a good night's sleep." I immediately thought of the years spent in the same environment in Ramle with all the beds along the walls and someone telling me to go to sleep. Surely the world contained something different! Then no sooner had we got to sleep when this burly bloke who smelled of cow dung was making a terrible din and urging us to get up and get ready for milking. It was still dark and if I had had a watch, which you know I didn't, then I would have known it was four thirty a.m.

We learned how to walk behind cows that knew more of what was happening than we did, and we learned to be careful where we trod, for there are disgusting piles of cow droppings for the unsuspecting in the night. And we learned how to let the cows go into the stalls that they wanted to and how to attach the milking cups, and that we had to do it over and over and over for the next week. During this time, we were briefed about how there would be an allocation of employment and the city boys went off to somewhere else never to be seen again. After about a week, myself and another boy were given the option of work on a dairy farm at Camden and a sheep and cattle station near Canberra. We both stood deliberating this huge decision and almost together we indicated our preferences. I think his name was Les and he opted for the dairy farm, and after a week of stupid hours and walking in cow shit, I wanted the sheep and cattle station. I am sure that I got the better deal. Soon after, I was loaded into a van with all my gear and driving into Sydney City to the Salvation Army building, given a train ticket, shown the night desk and wished all the best for my life in Australia. Up until now I was under the impression that English was the spoken language.

CHAPTER TEN

ARRIVING AT LANYON

At the Central Railway Station by four thirty in the morning to catch the train at seven. A slight piece of excessive "time safety factor" but there was a very good reason. The night in the Salvation Army digs was one to forget and not only because it was cold and I had no idea of the time. There were smells there that I still cannot identify today, some of them from the bodies that lurked in every nook and cranny and some that I think were built into the building to identify its use. And there are whiskery people who look shrivelled up and don't talk but rather mumble at me with eyes that clearly distrust this fresh-faced young man who is invading their space. No way of knowing the time, dozing fitfully during a long cold night, wondering if the whiskery ones ate young boys, and the fear of missing my train meant that I awoke early and followed the instruction sheet and walked to the station somewhat early. If I knew then what I know now, I would not have ventured out at that time of day and on foot for anyone or anything.

Railway stations in the mid-sixties were always filled with people. Porters, passengers, ticket sellers, newsagents and more whiskery people who didn't look as scary on the station. There was the smell of steam trains and this could have been any large station in England. I asked one person who was dressed in railway garb where I should go to catch the train to Queanbeyan and he looked at me as if I had two heads. He turned to his "mate" and they spoke in a foreign tongue and then spoke to me and gestured at the same time. I immediately reverted to plan B and showed them the ticket squashed firmly in my sweaty little palm. I must have looked like a real fool as he gestured and spoke, but I was obviously not getting the message and so he reverted to his back-up plan and wrote the platform number on my ticket and pointed. Strange people these Australians, no one speaks English, but everything is written in English.

I still had my sixteen pounds and with a series of gestures and slow talking I managed to get some breakfast and a magazine to read. I settled back to wait for the train and hoped that I wouldn't fall asleep on the waiting room bench. The big railway clock took an hour to move each minute until eventually a porter with a hooked pole pulled down the names of the towns for my train and there before me was the name Queanbeyan along with Bungendore, Yass, and Goulburn. Can you imagine a sixteen-year-old Geordie trying to pronounce those names?

The train arrived and I struggled on with my huge suitcase and settled into a seat with the case beside me. I probably could have put the case in the baggage car but had no idea how to and probably would not have been understood. Sleep started to settle in my drowsy head until I snapped back to wide awake. What if I miss my stop? How long does it take? What were the stations before? I should have written them down, and how could I get anyone to make sure that I got off in Queanbeyan when I couldn't talk to anyone? So, I made myself stay awake and watched each station as they arrived, always ready to jump off if I spotted my stop. I may have dozed but never slept, and what I thought might have taken an hour or so must have taken closer to five, and by the time I saw QUEANBEYAN on the station sign, I was hungry, tired, and at the end of my tether, but wearily lugged my suitcase out of the carriage and stood on the platform amidst the grime and steam and noise of the station.

A chap looking a lot like a ferret busily shuffled towards me. He wore what was once a hat but was now a series of leather looking bits held together by a hatband and flopping down on one side to cover one ear. His shirt and trousers were covered in dust and the pants were held up by a belt that could have tethered an elephant, whilst his elastic-sided boots looked as if they would fall off when he walked and that's why he shuffled. As bad as he seemed to me, I can now imagine what I looked like to him and that's probably how he twigged immediately who I was. I was so smug in my hobnail boots, skin-tight green and gold pinstriped jeans and Newcastle football jumper. Just how stupid I must have looked. He didn't make any comment however, and simply strode over and introduced himself as "Bunny Ooze", shook my hand vigorously, grabbed my suitcase and strode off the platform. Having no choice, because he had all my possessions, I followed on behind with my hobnails making me sound and look like a cross between a poor tap dancer and an ice skater. By the time I'd clicked and slipped outside, my new companion had thrown my case into the tray of an old yellow Dodge truck and was waiting for me to climb in.

We drove sedately through the town of Queanbeyan, a town that I thought was caught in a time warp, and then out onto the Monaro Highway. After a while on this single lane but well-maintained road we turned off onto the Tharwa Road, which was referred to as a gravel road but in fact was corrugated dirt with potholes randomly spaced for variation. The old truck rattled and I was sure that parts of it would simply fall off and that the whole vehicle would slide sideways into the field, or should I say paddock. I wasn't au fait with these terms yet. No seatbelts in those days to prevent the carnage, just this mad Australian driver who could sort of drive, roll a cigarette, talk, laugh, and look everywhere whilst pointing to various landmarks and trying to explain them in his foreign tongue. I later found out that he was one of the slower drivers on the station. If this was the slower of them it's no wonder they needed a strong immigration policy, for the death rate must have been huge.

After about an hour of driving, and I use that term loosely, we slid to a halt in a cloud of dust which cleared and we were parked inches in front of a big white gate with LANYON printed on a wooden sign, and just behind was a cubby house with a sliding door which turned out to be the mailbox. I looked at Bunny and he looked at me and I understood from his gestures that he wanted me to open the gate. It was probably a good thing that I couldn't understand the words that he used at that time. I am not an idiot and my sixteen-year-old brain had mastered Pythagoras' Theorem, but the mechanics of this gate had me stumped. He slid out of the truck and deftly removed the chain without undoing all of the fencing wire that I was struggling with and allowed the gate to swing open. He drove through and I closed the gate after it swung open a couple of times while I grabbed at the chain. The last mile was past a series of cottages, all with whitewashed walls and green roofs, until we arrived at a group of buildings and came to a halt in another cloud of dust.

All of these buildings were white and green as if there was a huge special on those coloured paints, but everything was clean and tidy. There was a room that I later identified as the smoko room with lots of men sitting around eating and talking. My driving companion, who I later learned was called Bernie Hughes, had removed my case from the Dodge and had driven off to what looked like a machinery shed, leaving me standing in the road with my suitcase and stupid clothes on a sheep and cattle station twelve thousand miles from what had been home, unable to speak the language and feeling utterly alone. Welcome to the land of opportunity. Cousin James had a lot to answer for at that moment.

Luckily, a sophisticated gentleman with white moleskin trousers and green jumper—it must have been coincidence— emerged from a doorway that a midget would have struggled to exit from. It turned out that he was Mr Murdoch McGregor Giekie who was the manager of the property and vehemently denied any Scottish ancestry. He did speak words that I could understand however which was a huge relief, and he guided me to a small room on the end of another white and green building which was to be my home for the next four years.

My room was about four meters square with a single bed, chest of drawers, table with one chair, and a huge open fireplace. He told me to put my stuff away and report back to the office from which he emerged. And so started the most wonderful four years of my life to date. A time when I learned to enjoy my environment, and when I looked forward to every day with a passion, found the closest thing yet to a family, and eventually fell in love and married my soulmate, with whom I still share my life.

Lanyon Pty Ltd was a sheep and cattle station of approximately ten thousand acres located South of Canberra near the small town of Tharwa. It had some two hundred and fifty acres of lucerne and was bordered on its western boundary by the Murrumbidgee River and stretched almost to the Monaro Highway on the eastern boundaries. It was first occupied as early as 1828 by one Timothy Beard, an ex-convict arriving in

Australia in 1806 who was forced out of the area by land grants when James Wright and John Hamilton Mortimer Lanyon settled as squatters in 1833. It is a real coincidence that one of my newfound friends who has remained a friend ever since is called John Hamilton. Lanyon returned to the UK in 1841 and Wright was forced to sell the property to Andrew Cunningham, who with his brother James eventually acquired other properties in the area, including Tuggeranong.

In 1921, after James's death, Lanyon was sold to Harry Osborne of Currandooley near Bungendore, who in turn sold it to Thomas Field in 1930. By the time I had arrived, it was still owned by the Field family, but with the exception of one unforgettable day, I was lucky enough not to be of their acquaintance.

CHAPTER ELEVEN

THEY SPEAK 'STRINE

My first afternoon and I still cannot understand a thing that is said to me. The two chaps who I was with were really nice and I'm sure that they would help me out but they look pretty intimidating. One looks to be about two hundred and his clothes might be older. He has a silver five o'clock shadow and a rolly hanging from the corner of his mouth that constantly needs to be relit and causes him to cough and fart at the same time. His clothes are the same as Bernie's and I assume he goes to the same tailor or disposal store. His name is Charlie and I never will understand him, but neither does anyone else except his wife and kids. The other is a burly, jovial chap who also has a five o'clock shadow and wears the same spectacles as I do. His forearms are enormous and I get the impression that he is the more commanding of the two. And so, I met Charlie Preston and Les Perrott.

Our task was, with the aid of a hoe, to remove Bathurst Burr from as much of the paddock that we drove to in the allotted time. We parked under some old gum trees and I was given my hoe and a quick demonstration of Bathurst Burr removal. My understanding of their strange tongue was never going to be enough but off I went wielding my hoe at anything that moved in the breeze. Les has since recounted my efforts of that afternoon and tells me that I did actually hit some Burr along with Saffron

Thistle, Scotch Thistle, tussocks and good old edible grass. He also told me that I worked like a dervish and he thought that I might actually turn out all right with the correct training and if I learned to speak English. How ironic.

Late in the afternoon I was summoned back to the Land Rover and we went back to the smoko room where they collected their saddle bags, smiled, and after a brief cheerio went home. I slowly unravelled the events of my first day and after scrutinising the blisters on my hands, I concluded that I was now a working man and not the skinny, pommie, paper boy that I was that morning. Assuming that I was finished for the day, I wandered off to my little room, unpacked all my worldly possessions into drawers, and sat on the end of my bed with a million questions to be answered. At this point in time, I may have broken down and cried for only the second time in my life, but before I could feel sorry for myself my door was flung open and this cockney apparition with a smile from ear to ear walked bow-legged into my new domain, and said in perfect cockney English with a touch of Lancastrian drawl, "Gerday, I'm John and I'm in the room next door."

There are some friendships which withstand the test of time and despite lengthy absences they resume unabated as if no parting took place. This is the type of friendship that developed between John Hamilton and myself and I hope that it shall remain so for the rest of our lives. John was shorter and stockier than me both then and now and we shared a passion for soccer. We rarely got to work together except in the cattle or sheep yards but we could talk for hours over dinner or at smoko and I never tired of his company. On that first night he showed me our bathroom, which was about fifty yards from our rooms, the dining room, and kitchen, and introduced me to the cook and housekeeper, helped me light the open fire in my room, and we carted armfuls of wood into the rooms for the night burning. We ate a huge dinner and chatted for ages before I needed to sleep so badly that I crashed in mid-sentence. Strangely I slept like a log that night and having no idea of time, I was surprised by John shaking me to consciousness with a, "Come on Robin, time to get breakfast, we have to be at work by seven."

A quick shower and into those stupid work clothes, downed a big breakfast and off to the smoko room. After a while they were all gathered and chatting, with John acting as interpreter. He assured me that I would soon come to grips with the Australian accent and in all honesty I did. Mr Giekie turned up shortly after me and introduced me to all the men. "This is Robin Reed who comes from Yorkshire in England. Robin this is Ted Wheeler, Bernie Hughes, who you have met, and Les Perrott and Charlie Preston. These others are Tom Price and Joe Manley, and of course you've met young John." There was one other person on the property and that was old Eric the gardener, who rarely was seen by anyone unless something was wrong in his garden. All of these people lived and worked on the property except for Ted who, with his wife, ran and lived in the Post Office at Tharwa, a small village some two miles away.

Mr Giekie allocated all the jobs, and off everyone went to busy themselves: Les and Charlie off mustering, Bernie off to his rabbiting job, Joe back to grooming, Tom and John went to a workshop, and Ted and I were to feed the stock.

He got me gloves, side cutters, and a hook on a stick, the same as the ones used in shearing sheds to move bales of wool, and we went to the machinery shed and he started up the big brother of the dodge that I had arrived in. Dotted across the property were hay sheds full of bales of lucerne hay. They were the old-style small rectangular bales with wire ties and varied in weight from bloody heavy to feather light. Our job was simple; we went to a shed and loaded up bales and drove to various paddocks, and after cutting the ties we spread the hay for the stock to eat. Can't get easier than that, can it? Even the simplest of tasks can have their "ups and downs" and I mean that literally. At the sheds I was the un-stacker and Ted the stacker, that is he packed them onto the trucks. This never varied in all the weeks that we fed out and the reason was simple. Ted was the boss, and I wasn't, and he didn't want all of the little surprises that are found in haystacks like brown snakes, rats, mice, rabbits, and even the occasional feral cat. Once the truck was loaded and we got to the drop off point, I climbed onto the back, cut the wire ties, and threw the hay off for the stock, making sure that the wire didn't get dropped with the hay. Ted drove along slowly, whilst I did this, again because he was the boss. And so, my first winter went by and I learned to speak Strine, how to maintain my balance perched on top of a load of hay that was rocked perilously close to overturning, how to use the hook to turn bales at the bottom of stacks and dodge whatever was hidden under them, and how to open and close the thousands of gates that we passed through. But I learned even more important things like where each paddock was and what stock there was on the property. And I learned that these country people were warm and friendly, and that the clothes that they wore were far more suitable than the kit that I had turned up in, and that I loved open fireplaces and the sound of rain on an iron roof, and all of the stories that Ted told me were fascinating and that when I grew up, I could drive the truck, one day. The irony was that this old feller that took me through the first Aussie winter was called Ted and even bore a slight resemblance to my stepfather. I did have other jobs in that first winter, such as fencing, drenching, learning to milk, laying fox baits, cutting suckers, and a million other things, but the drunken balancing act perched five tiers up on the back of a lurching ten-ton truck was what stuck in my memory.

And so, I learned that Australians spoke English and I spoke Australian and that if we all spoke slowly then with only a modicum of interpretation we could get by. By the time I turned seventeen I had a full set of real clothes and even had a good hat, but it wasn't "broken in" yet because it still looked like a hat. I have often thought later about this and other periods in my life, and it has occurred to me that each time I became comfortable with my existence it was at a time when I was insulated in a cocoon type way with the bounds of my world well defined and therefore easy to digest and be comfortable with. Lanyon was indeed a comfortable place for me to be and for the next four years I was to be as "at home" as never before.

My first job cutting Bathurst Burr, and other unsuspecting plants, was my introduction to Les Perrott, and soon after my arrival at Lanyon, John took me to meet Les's family and I was welcomed into their home with open arms and a warmth that I could not quite comprehend at that time and may have appeared shy and reticent to them. They were a family who could interact with each other, sometimes in argument and others in shared laughter and shared activities. It was initially very difficult to come to terms with this concept and I probably seemed a little withdrawn and standoffish. What I was experiencing, for the first time, was probably quite normal family interaction. Not always pleasant but always as a group. They ate as a family and although I believe that it wasn't always the case they talked as they ate and shouted and bickered and laughed and did it as a family. Les's wife is Beryl, and she was always, and still is, a happy-go-lucky person who in those days enjoyed a beer and a smoke and an old-fashioned barbeque. They had four children at the time. Clarence the eldest was about a year younger than me, Patricia thirteen, Robert eleven, and the youngest Ian aged seven-ish. I can never get them all correct. From my first introduction I was made welcome, and although we have had our disagreements, I remain still a part of their family group. Les and Beryl had another daughter soon after my arrival whose name is Lorraine. Each of these people have a place in my story and will be mentioned often as part of my life.

CHAPTER TWELVE

THE STOCKMAN

The first winter was over and on one fine and warm spring morning Mr Giekie when allocating tasks asked me if I could ride. It took a short time for me to understand that he was asking if I could ride a horse and not a number nine bus or pushbike. So obviously I replied that I could. If I had realised that he meant a horse then it may have been a different response, but I had watched Les and Charlie riding and it didn't look that hard.

"OK then, you can go with Les and muster Big Monks." I had learned something of the paddocks and was aware that Big Monks was basically a creek with big banks on either side that climbed almost vertically to each fence line. It was somewhere that Ted and I would feed out just inside the gate because we couldn't drive the truck up the track.

Now the truth was that I had seen horses before. Anyone living next door to a major racecourse had to have seen them. And even more encouraging was that I had once ridden a Shetland pony on a trip to Scarborough with an uncle called Tom and his wife Alice. I didn't really ride the pony but rather sat on it whilst the owner walked it up and down the sand and my feet dragged along the ground. Not the most perfect training for what I was about to do, I will admit, but I learned one thing about being an Aussie and that was that you can have a go at anything. The other thing in my favour was that Les was wise enough to know that I had never ridden before, which could be explained by my total lack of nous when confronted with saddle and bridle.

My trusty steed was called Dolly and we were to become partners over the next four years. She probably didn't suspect at this stage that I wasn't as clever as her. Les showed me how to put bridle and saddle on with the cropper under the tail, surcingle and girth strap tightened twice, and how to stretch out the front leg to stop the girth strap from rubbing. It should be noted that Dolly was the quietest horse ever to work sheep and cattle, she never played up even when being broken in and didn't have a bad bone in her body. But she had probably never had such an idiot riding her before. Holding the reins as instructed, I climbed into the saddle and sat there as if it was the major achievement of the day and those reins were probably pulling her chin back into her chest until instructed to give them some slack.

And so, with Les in the lead, off we went to muster the sheep in Big Monks. My riding prowess must have caused Les some amusement because I thought that every move that Dolly made was an attempt to unseat me and I spent the first five minutes whoaing and giddy-upping, and Les to his credit simply kept reassuring and instructing until I got the hang of sitting on top and letting the horse walk along beside Les's horse, a beautiful dapple grey called Princess. I sat and watched as we passed through gates and Les opened and shut them without dismounting which I thought then was quite clever. I didn't know then that this was a man who had mustered in the Snowy Mountains, ran in Brumbies in the mountains around Tumbarumba and spent almost all of his life sitting on and breaking in horses, opening and shutting gates was a doddle.

And so I learnt about rein length and using the knees and not leaning forward and all sorts of other things, none of which prepared me for Big Monks.

Down through the Bullock Paddock into Little Bandicoot and then Big Monks gate just above Bandicoot yards. I looked ahead and could only see mountains, whereas in truth they were just big hills, and Dolly took this opportunity to shake which almost unseated me, but I wasn't concerned like I would have been ten minutes earlier. "Follow me and let the horse pick her own way, and don't rein in too tightly, and use your knees to stay on, and if you really need to, there is the monkey to hang on to, but you won't need it." Wonderful words of wisdom but I was damned if I could see any monkey to hang on to and wouldn't appear stupid by asking.

My right foot was about two feet off the side of the hill and my left was about five feet above the low side and the track that we followed was a sheep track. Now even I knew that sheep are only about two foot six tall, and Dolly and I were about seven feet tall, which meant that there were trees and bushes that kept on trying to rip my head and shoulders off, and even fat sheep weren't as wide as Dolly and me so there were trees and rocks that tried to rip my legs off. I didn't do one tiny bit of mustering but watched incredulously as Les and Princess scrambled up shaly banks and crossed gullies after they had completely disappeared in them, and all the while Dolly and I followed like a drover's dog. Speaking of dogs, I was also astounded at the work of Les's dogs and in particular one called Bow. He was a Collie/Barb cross and what he could do was incredible. After some time we miraculously ended up back at the gate into Little Bandicoot and I had survived my initiation to being a stockman.

By the time we were there Mr Giekie and some others had set up the yards to drench the ewes prior to them going in with the rams. I dismounted and my legs folded under me like two jelly sticks and whilst not hairy before, the inside of my legs were now hairless and red raw. But I felt an elation that is indescribable and was truly disappointed when told that we didn't have to take the sheep back into their hills but rather we would just let them back through the gate and they would find their own way home. There was one more treat for me and that was the counting of the sheep through the gate. Les instructed me to pick up some twigs and when he shouted "hundred" I was to keep tally by transferring twigs between hands. Les would be the first to tell you that he wasn't that keen on the school books but the way he counted sheep was incredible. Holding the gate and with Bow gently keeping the sheep moving, he counted in twos and threes with his cry of "hundred" loud and clear with me responding "one", "two", and so on.

Luckily for me, the need to feed hay to the stock had passed and I was to spend more and more time working with stock, and Dolly was my horse to look after and I did just that, and even on Sundays I would take her treats whilst she was in the Horse Paddock. After each day was over, I would wash her down and brush her meticulously before riding again. We became a team and I felt like I had become a valuable part of the stockman team and looked forward to each day's work.

Going into summer the other men would prepare for the harvesting of the lucerne paddocks. There were about two hundred and fifty acres of lucerne and some were to have irrigation equipment installed before I left. Once harvesting started there would be around-the-clock work for Ted, John, and Tom, and I occasionally was required to do some raking. But for most of the time I was mustering and doing stock work.

I learned that being a "pommie bastard" was indeed a term of endearment, at least in my case, and that being a "hobbity hoy" was being a hairy arsed boy, and that Flag Ale came in "long necks", and it was fun to swim in the Murrumbidgee River on a warm summer afternoon, and the smell of newly mown hay is intoxicating, and a million other things. During that first summer I would sit on the banks of the river under the shade of Mount Tennant and make up poetry in my head and dream of one day writing it and putting it into a book. It was the first time that the thought of writing came upon me. I wish I had listened to myself then!

Work was hard and the week included Saturday morning, but I would have worked seven days a week if it was required. It was as close to slave labour as I've been, and I didn't care. Saturday mornings were spent mainly in Mr Giekie's garden with John Hamilton and it is amazing that anything grew there at all. The poison strengths for weeds were at best guessed and its application was somewhat haphazard, but apart from one old beech tree, nothing seemed to have any long-term effects. Another of the Saturday morning jobs was watering the trees that the landscape gardeners planted down the main driveway from the Tharwa road, to the homestead. With a huge water tank on the big yellow International we would start up the pump and go from tree to tree with water splashing everywhere over the person on the back operating the pump. Great fun in the summer with the temperature in the mid-thirties. Then on my day off I would work on my saddle and bridle or go for walks in the paddocks or go for drives in John's car or just hang out at Les and Beryl's. Perhaps the only things missing from my life were the blond hair, freckles, and a dog called Lassie, and although you may feel a little nauseous at this idyllic and tranquil scene, I really was absolutely happy.

Of course there were times when even I got frustrated with the heat and the mob not moving along and the dogs looking for the shade because all of these were also part and parcel of stock work. I had acquired three dogs for my second summer and they were the most diverse bunch that there could be. Old Ted had given me a doe eyed little Kelpie bitch called Biddie and even Les said she was as good a yard dog as he had ever seen, and indeed he asked to keep her when I was conscripted. The second was a dog that Les gave me called Spin. He was a red bitser who got his name from chasing his tail, a most annoying habit when you are trying to work sheep, but when he did work, he was a good honest toiler of a dog. The third was a Collie/Barl cross and the son of Les's dog Bow. I called him Pedro because as a small pup he was always sleeping in the shade, but a more inappropriately named dog, never there was. Pedro knew more than any human being and would often incur the wrath of wiser stockmen than I whilst still managing to achieve the objective. One thing that Pedro taught me was that wherever I went he could bring a mob to me. I learned a whole new vocabulary with my dogs and one tirade that I learned still is vivid today. "Insert name of dog, you up stumped, jumped, never come down, wall eyed, mongrel bred, insert colour of dog bastard, get behind here." Every dog on Lanyon knew that off by heart.

Les taught me better things than that as well and they are still relevant to anyone trying to control a dog today. If you can get your dog to "sit and come" then you have control over the dog and can teach anything after that. The other thing that he taught me was that as I couldn't speak English for so long, then neither can dogs understand English. It is pointless saying to your dog, "I would like you to remain in the position of having you bum on the ground whilst I count these sheep into the yards and then you can go and have a drink." He simply does not understand a thing. Teach him to sit and stay and you will have achieved the result.

CHAPTER THIRTEEN

MORE SCARY MOMENTS

I learned many invaluable lessons during my time at Lanyon, some of which served me for years to come whilst others were directed at making my work easier and less painful. Some lessons needed no reinforcement and others were driven home with the force of a 0-10-0 freight locomotive. During the summer months we often left early to muster paddocks so that the drenching or whatever could be finished in the cool of the day. I had been told a thousand times that a hat and fresh, clean water were as much a part of life as the stockwhip and saddle, but in some things, I was a slow learner. Well into summer and I had the poorest excuse for a hat that ever there was, and I always seemed to forget that icy cold bottle of water in the fridge as I grabbed my lunch.

One particular day we had left early to muster a mob of wild and woolly wethers, from their hideout in the hills. Even with Les, Charlie, and myself, we had troubles getting them together and into the yards, and so the morning heat was well and truly upon us by the time drenching started. Mr Giekie had all-hands-on-deck, and we were slowly but surely working our way through the mob. The problem was that the dogs had decided that enough was enough and they still had the job of getting the sheep back to their paddock, and so they were allowed some rest time whilst the humans filled the races. Each raceful was less packed than the last. The way that I would drench was to get in the race and work from back to front so that all of the sheep were the right way around at the gate. Using a small handheld "kettle drum" gun I was making good progress but was also starting to become frustrated, tired, and very vocal with all of these ***###!!! sheep.

No water, dehydration, loss of concentration, sun stroke, and a half full race of big woolly cantankerous wethers, and the recipe was complete. I turned to drench the next one and it wasn't there. Instead, it was covering the five or so bounds needed to butt me in the chest with horns like a high country billygoat, and the gap closed faster than any reaction that I could make. I don't know how anyone found my glasses and how they were still intact was a miracle of science, but they were about the only "intact" things around. I had been walked on, peed on, pebbled on, and sat on by wethers running from one end of the race to the other. John was trying to get me out of there only to have a wether head-butt him, and eventually I was extracted and placed in the back of the Land Rover.

I remember being asked that age-old question of, "Are you OK?" and there was no doubt that I was not, which became evident when trying to stand only induced violent vomiting and loss of consciousness. Mr Giekie decided that I should be "checked out" and so he simply closed the back of the Land Rover and took me to Queanbeyan Hospital where I stayed for the next ten days.

Other words of wisdom that I obviously had trouble with were "Let the horse pick its own way." In another life my horse Dolly was probably a Buddhist Monk, she was so quiet and deliberate in everything, some would have called her slow, but I thought of her as efficient. She rarely made a wrong decision with her footing and I was the culprit who caused her to fall when, had I listened to wiser people, then both horse and rider would not have been injured. We were on our way back to the homestead after an innocuous day of lamb riding and a large rock loomed up in front of us with sheep tracks above and below it. There was no obvious reason to venture above or below the rock and so when she decided to take the low road I should have just sat there for the ride, but no I was the boss and I decide which way we'll go. When she was ready to place her hoof on the ground, she suddenly had her head wrenched up the hill and missed the ground all together. Luckily, we were almost on the flats and it only took a couple of rolls for us to come to a rest, with me still in the saddle but facing downhill and praying that she wouldn't keep rolling. Once again, she showed her worth and just lay there until I extracted myself from under her. Then she stood up and I was able to inspect for damage. She had bark off her head but otherwise appeared fine and apart from a soreness in my left leg I too felt fine. It was only when I tried walking that I realised that my left leg was about twice its normal size. So Dolly and I made our way back to the homestead where I bathed her gashes and rashes, and then Mr Giekie drove me off to Queanbeyan Hospital where I recuperated for the next few days.

Every day there was the potential for something to go wrong and how there weren't more serious injuries I don't know. They had horse-breakers who would come from Sydney to break in the young horses and then they would leave, and the stockmen would inherit these half-walked, half-talked nags and try to turn them into valuable stock horses. One batch broke one breaker's legs when she threw herself and her rider onto the ground, one bucked so violently that she threw Mr Giekie the full length of the reins and caught him and threw him again, and I doubt that his social life was much for weeks afterwards.

Another one threw its rider when he was trying to open a

gate and then proceeded to kick out one of his testicles from its protective pouch, and the one that broke the breaker's leg once threw Les, and it was so quick he literally was riding one minute and standing next to the horse the next. But the scariest moment for me was the verballing I got for something that I didn't do.

The owners of Lanyon would visit every now and then and generally, apart from a distant glimpse, John and I would have no contact. They also liked to spell their racehorses at Lanyon and one in particular, which was evidently something of a champion trained by one Mr Harry Plant in Sydney. Valiant Lad was in the middle of one of these spells and Mr T.A. Field himself was visiting. I had been given the job of running the "Lad" in each day and putting his coat on. I say that I had been given the job but in truth I thought it to be fun rather than a chore. Each day I would open the gate into his night yard and give him feed and fresh water, brush him down and put his coat on. Yes, every day at four o'clock and I was absolutely diligent in this.

It was an absolutely perfect Sunday afternoon and Pat had come with me to rug and feed the racehorse. We had gone to do this quite early because we could get some quiet time to sit and talk and maybe, you know, hold hands and stuff. As four o'clock approached we were about to let Valiant Lad in the yard when there came the most foulmouthed and abusive tirade from behind the laneway that we were sitting in.

To say that I was taken aback was an absolute understatement, and I could not begin to write the things that Mr Field was suggesting that Pat and I were allegedly doing and therefore not doing. No matter how I protested about it at the time, and my good and most honourable intentions, he only seemed to find new levels of obscenity and threat until I thought he may well have turned red and died. I decided that retreat was now the best option and with Pat in tow I raced off and fixed up his racehorse. As we sped off down the paddocks, we were left with the final threat that by Monday I would be off the place and lucky if I wasn't flogged within an inch of my life or hung, drawn, and quartered at the very least. Pat was in tears and I believed that this idyllic life that I had been experiencing was to be cut short with effect first thing Monday morning.

Monday, seven o'clock, and I'm in the smoko room waiting for the sack and shitting razorblades. Mr Giekie arrives and started the job allocations and still nothing. How can this man be so cruel? Then he allocates my job to go with Les and muster cattle and still no bollocking. Perhaps he's going to take me aside and not roar at me in front of everyone, the man's got heart after all, but no, nothing, he just wanders off to his office. I'm a wreck by now and knowing that old Ted is pally with T.A. Field, I ask if he has heard anything. No, nothing. But he does let me know that T.A. does enjoy some of Scotland's finest and was probably "in his cups" and had forgotten all about it by the time he got back to the homestead or indeed probably got a huge laugh about this little pommie bastard taking off like a rabbit. For the first time in my life, I felt something like an intense dislike for another human being and I use that term loosely. I have read many astonishing tales from Australia's colourful history and that man was the closest that I could ever imagine to the original arsehole squatter.

CHAPTER FOURTEEN

JBH, LBJ, AND LCP

A strange title you might be thinking; let me explain. There were three people who had a profound influence on my life during Lanyon, and indeed for the rest of my life, and they all had the most different of backgrounds. John Bailey Hamilton, Lyndon Baines Johnson, and Leslie Clarence Perrott.

As I have already mentioned, John Hamilton was an ex Little Brother who had travelled to Australia a couple of years before me and had worked on Lanyon since then. He was, and still is, an extremely uncomplicated character who has a wonderful ability to fit into almost every situation. I am sure he would be capable of high tea with the gentry as easily as he would be with a stubby, or in John's case a Scotch, and a sausage sandwich at a barbeque. He made me feel at home when I first arrived in Australia and was always there if I was feeling down or confused. After he bought his car, he took me everywhere he went and we holidayed together for those years at Lanyon. John left Lanyon shortly after I was conscripted and joined the then PMG, but I am sure he would have left anyway and moved on to other things.

John and I shared a passion for football, sorry—soccer, and we both played for the Queanbeyan Macedonian club. It was hard work balancing training and playing with our heavy workload at Lanyon, but John never once complained about driving us to training on those cold Canberra nights. We were two of only three players not of Macedonian extract, with the other being an Irish chap who was much older than us but we all three shared a joke and spoke in broad accents that no one else understood, which was only fair because all the others would speak Greek or Double Dutch. Our love for the game was not enough to make us continue however when the club brought a "really good" player from Europe somewhere to play, and he was rushed into the team at John's expense. No training or familiarisation, just arrived on Thursday, playing Saturday, and dropped John off the list without a by-your-leave. I complained bitterly about such things as loyalty and that we had made huge sacrifices to attend training and games but was met with a stony glare. And so, we said stick your club up your arse and left. A short time after, we were contacted by the coach who asked if we would come back because the Irish chap had moved to another club and the "really good" player turned out to be as useless as teats on a bull. We graciously declined.

John and I along with some of the Perrott kids would head off to Batemans Bay nearly every weekend in summer, and he was always the driver unless Les and Beryl took us. We would sometimes stay overnight in an old boat shed at Batehaven with sleeping bags and it was quite scary. There were paddle boats that we splashed around in and time to laze around in the sun, and fish and chips and walks along the rocks. On one occasion we walked too far and found that the tide had come in and blocked our way back to the beach. The only way out was to climb the cliff back to the road and walk. Luckily, it wasn't sheer, and we all made it back, but Patricia was pretty scared whilst we heroes pretended that we weren't. On the way back to Lanyon we would stop at the Paragon Café in Braidwood and have a huge meal and milkshakes and listen to the jukebox. The trip from the Bay back to Lanyon could take forever in those days because they still had the ferry at Nelligen, which on a busy weekend could take hours to get across.

John had a Vauxhall Velox as his first car and as I said he would take me everywhere that he went and he taught me to drive in it. When we were still playing football one of the games was at Cooma and as the club didn't have a team bus everyone had to find their own way to the games. I had my L plates and John just jumped into the passenger side and told me to drive. I had already spent time in the Lanyon vehicles but this was the first time that I was to drive on the road. He had patience beyond that which I could imagine as we crawled down the Monaro Highway towards Cooma. "You can go a little faster if you want" was all that he said, and he had allowed a time safety factor to ensure that we got to the game on time. We did get there on time and I played a screamer and was totally buggered after the game. To my surprise, John again jumped in the passenger seat and made me drive home. It is not a huge drive, but by the time we got home I was ready to sleep for a week.

John's first holiday while I was at Lanyon was on his own and he went up to Queensland and unfortunately had an accident in his car, which meant he had to leave it at Southport to be repaired. When it was ready to be picked up, I went with him "for the drive." A twenty-four-hour bus trip, straight to the repairers and pick up his car and drive straight back to Canberra. I still don't know how he did it but I was not able to drive then and he did it all himself. I remember coming across the Harbour Bridge and trying to stay awake and thinking that we still had six hours to go. No freeways in those days, and the Hume Highway was a single narrow-laned road.

Sometime around September/October 1966, there was a

buzz of excitement around the place, and we were told that the President of the USA was coming to visit. Of course he didn't really know me, although he was to have a profound effect on my life, but it was exciting to think that such an important person as him was to be on the property. For weeks beforehand the preparations were underway, with the landscapers from Leura swinging from trees as they pruned them, sprucing the entrances. The gardener and John and I were mowing and raking and trimming and raking the courtyard and other path areas.

Nearly the big day and huge marquees were erected, fences had another coat of white applied, and for ages I couldn't understand why but there were helicopters flying around the surrounding hills. It was all mind boggling. And when the big day came, I began to realise just what a huge "suck job" it all was.

Lyndon Baines Johnson was born on the 27th of August 1908 near the town of Stonewall in Texas in the good old USA. Being a Texan, he had a liking for good cattle and barbeques and being important. And he had many important functions in Australia and this was no doubt to be a good diversion, and some good PR never went astray. While he was at Lanyon, he would also plant a Dogwood tree amid much pomp and ceremony. But the good folk of Lanyon weren't going to be allowed to spoil his day to the point that one worker Joe Docen—I apologise if the spelling is wrong—was not allowed on the property that day because of his Dutch ancestry or some such ridiculous reason. All gates on the Tharwa road were locked to stop undesirables from getting on to the place and I believe that there were strange people positioned in the surrounding hills with high-powered rifles in case he was attacked by some crazed stockman armed with a handful of Hereford dung or something equally as dangerous. Les's daughter Patricia, who had started work, had to have special permission to go home afterwards, and John and I had to find our own lunch because we weren't allowed around the homestead or in the courtyard.

As I mentioned, the president, evidently, really was taken with cattle and so it was decided that we would line his approach to the homestead with mobs of our beautiful Hereford cattle so that he could go, ooh ahh, and stuff like that, and get a warm fuzzy feeling inside like he was on the ranch in Texas. I have no idea at what time he was to arrive but we were all sent out early in the morning to muster stock and hold them in prearranged locations. I was very lucky that my mob were from the Bullock Paddock and I was to hold them at the main gate, which was surrounded on three sides by fences and holding them there was fairly easy. At least for the first two hours it was, and then they decided that it was time to wander off and have a feed. And so, I spent the next two hours pushing them back to the allocated spot. Now I say that I was very lucky because I had this good area to hold them and I would be the first that he passed. On the other side of the road, Bernie had his mob with only two fences and his mob were giving him much grief after the first two hours and were almost impossible after another two hours. Les and Charlie had even worse areas to hold stock, with no defined fences but rather along the edge of the approach roads. When the entourage finally arrived, the cattle were being very naughty and breaking everywhere, which led to everyone galloping madly around and cracking stockwhips and swearing like bullockys. A long procession of vehicles, each with men in suits standing on the running boards, and looking everywhere at the same time, and the windows all wound tightly up with tinting so dark you could not have seen a bloody thing. They didn't slow down or wind the windows down and nobody later said thanks on his behalf or if he thought the stock were really good or kiss my arse or anything. As soon as they had passed, I wheeled Dolly round and at a full gallop we raced back to the stables, which unfortunately meant that we overtook the President as he made his way to the homestead. I didn't think that this was a problem but the powers to be did.

Mr Giekie must have been advised that his ruffian stockman had given the President's security people quite a scare by galloping past his cavalcade, and he informed me that I had been very naughty, and didn't I realise that they may have taken some protective action against me. I thought about it later and maybe they could have shot me or arrested me or something. All I wanted to do was get back to my room and get into some comfortable gear and have a beer. But I couldn't even get to the fridge.

Meanwhile, along the main entrance, there was the sound of revelry and the smell of barbequed food and the huge marquees were full of people all sucking up to LBJ or just trying to get to say G'day to him so that they could mention it in their social circles. "Yes, the president and I had lunch together the other day at that quaint little cattle property near Tharwa. Oh, he was so charming with his southern drawl and him surrounded by those beautiful yellow roses." They would get much social mileage from this whilst LBJ convinced Prime Minister Holt to commit thousands of young Australians to make the Vietnam conflict appear more credible

And so, President Johnson planted a Dogwood tree on the lawn in front of Lanyon homestead, smiled nicely at the colonials, convinced Australia to fight a war of no logistic consequence, ate our tucker, and jumped back into his blackened car, and left via the new bitumen road that the people of Tharwa had been trying to have sealed since the Queen's visit in nineteen fifty something or other.

We then got the job of cleaning up the area and went back to our normal daily routines. The Dogwood tree died slowly and the yellow roses were removed, probably to another function, and John and I learned a very good lesson about how useless the whole exercise had been for the good people who lived and worked on Lanyon station. The only thing that I gained from it was an invitation to join the Australian Army and go to Vietnam.

And so, to the third member of this triad—LCP. Leslie Clarence Perrott. Les was born and raised in the Tumbarumba area, where he gained an intimate knowledge of all things rural and in particular, he had an exceptional ability with horses. I have since lived in Tumbarumba and have seen some of the country that he rode and was amazed. If ever I needed a role model to become a stockman, then he was perfect for the job. He is a hard taskmaster but he also has a boisterous sense of humour and never seemed to find any task too hard or any situation beyond him. This was never more apparent than my first Christmas with the Perrott family.

Christmas had been many things to me over my life so far and to say that I hadn't enjoyed any of them would be a big fat lie, but there had always been something missing, and Christmas 1965 helped me understand a lot about Christmas and people.

I had now become part of Les and Beryl's extended family and was accepted into their home and way of life. I had become very comfortable there and was being treated as one of the family. Les always told people that I came for dinner one night and stayed forever. Anyway, as Christmas approached it was apparent that nobody had any money and that we therefore would have a very "lean" time of it. I became quite despondent because I wanted to show my appreciation for all that this family had done for me. No one else seemed to be too concerned however, and I was often reassured that it would all be all right.

As the big day approached Les took us into one of the paddocks and cut part off a wild cherry tree, which I must admit looked something like a good old fashioned Christmas tree. We took it back and put it in a bucket with bricks and soil and if watered every day it would hold up for a couple of weeks. And so we had the tree, but no decorations, or so I thought. I have found that nearly all Australian families have a box or boxes of decorations hidden under a bed or in a shed somewhere, and so did Beryl. We decorated the tree and the lounge room and what we didn't have we made from painted strips of newspaper which were coloured and made into chain streamers, milk bottle tops, and foil wrap. So, we now had a tree and decorations and could buy a few small presents which were again supplemented with things that we made like wrapping paper around a cardboard box for a kitchen tidy and a wooden box made from old pieces of wood that made a perfect ferret box and a billycart, again made from things just lying about. Whilst wrapping our home-made presents, I learned another Australianism, which at the time caused me some embarrassment. Patricia had wanted the Sellotape to finish a present and asked me to pass the Durex, which was evidently a brand of sticky tape, but in my language, it is the brand name of condoms. I was speechless and nobody could explain my disbelief that a young teenage girl was asking if I had a condom. So I sat there gawking and one of the boys grabbed the tape and passed it to her. Even when I realised the misunderstanding, I couldn't really explain that I thought she wanted a condom, so it only got worse and JBH had to quietly explain, and then Tricia was embarrassed but she took it well.

On Christmas morning Les got all of us boys in the car and we drove off and into Little Bandicoot paddock. He had his Mossberg shotgun and we crawled the last hundred yards to a position on the bottom side of the dam. Then quietly signalling to us to stay still, he crawled up the dam wall, took aim, and blasted enough ducks in one shot to feed everyone for Christmas dinner. Our job was to strip off and get into the dam to retrieve the ducks. Then back home and cleaned the ducks for Beryl to cook. We always had potatoes, pumpkin and spinach and Beryl and Patricia had made coloured jellies and homemade custard and produced a Christmas pudding that someone had given them. We feasted on wild duck and roasted vegetables with pudding, jelly, and custard, and we opened all of the presents whether homemade or bought, and it was by far and away the best Christmas Day that I had ever experienced. We were totally satisfied and no one complained about their present or the food or that we didn't have much money. It was what I believe is the essence of Christmas and was a lesson that I cannot forget. Even if we have the resources to buy all the things that we want at Christmas, it will not mean as much as sharing the time with the people you love the most.

Ian was still too young to go shooting and ferreting with the rest of us boys but Les would take us out or we would go by ourselves and spend hours roaming the paddocks catching rabbits and eradicating foxes. If Beryl wanted fish for dinner, then she would send us off down the river and we would always bring back a feed of trout or perch or cod. They were the days when the Murrumbidgee was in fact a river, and not the trickle we have turned it into today. There was always a vegetable garden with staple diet stuff like potatoes, pumpkin, corn, and beans, and they had a fresh billy of milk from the dairy each day, and the station provided mutton and beef and other vegetables from the homestead garden. John and I would sometimes nick peaches or apricots from the garden, and old Eric would be on the warpath and checking our thongs for footprints. We told him a thousand times that thongs were standard sizes and wouldn't prove guilt, but he knew it was us and wouldn't be put off by cheeky buggers like us.

Beryl and/or Patricia, when Beryl was ill with a bad back, would do all of our washing and we would all sit and watch television and chat at night. I still have a scar on my left "cheek" which Beryl gave me as I was being a smart arse and pointing my backside at her when she was ironing. "Go on," I said, "Iron me out." I had nylon swimming shorts on and copped a full burst of steam which left little round rings on my bum and they didn't go away. Another time as we watched telly, Beryl was passing out lollies and I said, "Toss one over" and she did. The problem was that the room was dark and I didn't see it until it was too late and it hit my glasses, shattering one lens, but thankfully I got nothing in my eyes. All of these interactions were things that had been alien to me until now.

And so, my time with the Perrotts developed to the point that I felt that this was my family and that it was something that I had never experienced before. The other thing that I was starting to experience was a strong feeling about Patricia, and before I left Lanyon that feeling was to become a love that has lasted to this day.

CHAPTER FIFTEEN

FROM STOCKMAN TO SWAGGY

The Field family had many properties that they could transfer stock to and from so that they could best utilise the available pastures, and during a particularly ordinary period they needed to move a large number of cattle from Lanyon to a property in the New England region near Armidale. The most efficient method of transport in those days was, apparently, by rail. Les was to accompany the stock on the train and I was to go for the experience and to be the one to run up and down beside the carriages each time the train had a stop.

I was over the moon with the thought of this trip and spent hours getting my gear together and asking Les what I should take, how long would we be away, what happens if the stock go down in the carriages, would we be in with the stock or in our own carriage, how would we cook our tucker, and he must have been so fed up with me but never got angry at all, at least not outwardly anyway. All the preparations were done and the big day was fast approaching.

The process was really quite simple, with the cattle being floated to the railway in Queanbeyan and loaded onto cattle trucks. Les and I were to be in with the guard in his van at the end of the train and then off we would go to Barrabri and unload them into yards and catch a train home again. There was obviously all sorts of paperwork and things to do but my role was to ensure that we didn't lose any cattle during the trip due to them getting down and stomped on by the others. So when the train stopped, I would jump off and run up and down with a prodder, just a big stick, and move them around to keep their circulation going and stop them jamming up in one corner.

Mr Giekie drove us to Queanbeyan, and we all supervised the loading, with me feeling really important counting cattle onto carriages and passing tallies to Les. I would climb around like a monkey opening and closing gates and waving my arms madly to push the right number into place. The noise was brilliant and I could almost imagine Wyatt Earp sitting on a fence at the railhead in Tombstone. It seemed to take forever but eventually everyone was happy with the numbers and how they were looking and we were ready to start off to Barrabri. Then the strangest thing happened and as I went to get the bags and swags to put in the guard's van the whistle sounded, and the train started to leave. Les and Mr Giekie had the strangest look on their faces and I imagine that Mr Giekie had visions of all Field's cattle being whisked off and he probably wished that Wyatt Earp was there. There followed a period of arm waving and heated discussion and assurances that we could beat the train to Tarago and board it there.

Into the stationmaster's car we piled and set off to race the train to Tarago. Without breaking any land speed records we cruised on through Bungendore and on, and were waiting on the station at Tarago when the train arrived. After transferring our kit and doing the first of many walks up and down the train we settled back in the guard's van and thought about a nice cuppa.

The guard was a kindly old chap who had this stove in the middle of his van and a small compartment with a bench type bed and skinny mattress on it, and Les and he soon had a good old conversation going over a steaming hot brew, which I suspect was made nicer with the addition of a dram or two from Mr Johnnie Walker. I think he enjoyed having some company for once, and although I didn't get to say much, I was a good listener and in my experience, the best way to be accepted by the older men was to listen attentively and ask questions with a wide eyed look as if it was the most important issue in the whole world. Sleeping was going to be a problem because there were no beds except for the guard's bench, but we had pillows and blankets and Les assured me that he had slept in worse conditions, and I was sure that he had. We had lots of tucker and could cook on the little stove in the middle of the van and if we needed to "go" there was a toilet that flushed, but I don't know where it flushed to, and it had a little sign advising not to use it in the station. All the comforts of home.

We stopped somewhere in the middle of nowhere and twice more in and around Sydney, and on each occasion the guard gave us an idea of how long we would be stopped for, and both Les and I would dash up and down the carriages prodding and cajoling the cattle to move around a bit without panicking them. After doing this three times the novelty had worn off somewhat and I was starting to get bored, tired, and wishing for my nice warm comfortable bed at Lanyon. Don't get me wrong, it was still very much an adventure but now it was into the part where the hero was doing it tough and things looked bleak. Like all good adventures, it would turn out all right.

It probably only took two nights to reach our destination although it seemed like two weeks and when we got to Barrabri, I must be honest and admit that train travel had lost a lot of its romance and charm. But here we were and without losing a single cow and they appeared to be in excellent health. Unloading started immediately and they were eased through a water point and counted with the tallies being exactly right. It was extremely dusty and hot and with all of the hollering and climbing fences and opening and shutting gates I was pretty thirsty. The stockmen who helped us unload offered us some longnecks which I gleefully accepted and Les, who normally never touched beer, had one as well. The beer was slightly warm, I was very hot and tired and the effect was almost instantaneous as I went from bouncing around everywhere to sitting in the shade half asleep. It was pleasant sitting in the yards half asleep while the world just ambled by in a hazy dream, but it wasn't the safest place to be and Les kicked me into action to grab the swags and got us a lift to the pub to get cleaned up, have a sleep, and prepare for the train home.

Les is not a great lover of a beer and I hadn't seen him indulge in many binges on anything alcoholic but had heard it rumoured that he enjoyed something called Rum and Green Ginger, and so when he offered to treat me later on, I felt really grown up to be in the presence of all these real stockmen and drinking some real grog and not just beer. Once again it was only a matter of time before I realised that I was out of my depth again and only the insistence of a more worldly mentor saved me from eradicating myself. Rum and Green Ginger have been removed from my list of social beverages and only once have I retried—and failed again. Clean, rested and on the train back home.

I slept like a baby all the way back to Sydney and Les woke me to get off at Hornsby so that we could visit with Beryl's sister and her family. Even though we had the opportunity to clean up before leaving Barrabri, we were still unshaven with dusty clothing that smelled of cows and had all of our extra clothes and things wrapped up in shirts and tied to sticks in the tradition of the Swagman, and we appeared to be drawing a lot of attention and were being avoided by most of the commuters as if we had the plague. Les thought it was hilarious that all these people could be so aghast at our appearance and was even more amused when Aunty Kath, who had only glimpsed us, panicked and called for her husband to come and deal with the two homeless-looking chaps coming down the side of the house. Neville came huffing and puffing around the corner unsure what to do or say and the relief on his face was priceless when he recognised Les. Kath and Neville are/were Salvoes and I think that was as close as Neville had come to allowing that bad word to slip out and Kath produced her best embarrassed laugh at the thoughts that passed through her brain. So, we had a hearty meal and continued the journey back to Lanyon and Les chuckled every time he thought of poor old Neville turning that corner with no idea of what to say to those two "homeless chaps."

Back home and the stories told and retold. I decided that the life of the drover might be romantic but transporting cattle by train was not to be my career ambition.

CHAPTER SIXTEEN

MAKE YOUR OWN FUN

There were very little tourist type attractions in and around Tharwa for we younger ones and as such we had to mostly make our own fun, which normally involved fishing, swimming, ferreting, shooting, and those type activities. The other "fun" we had was with the grown-ups who seemed to have an endless stream of visitors, and always with the accompanying party or barbeque. It seemed as if every weekend there would be a houseful of people at Les and Beryl's place and they would travel hundreds of miles to be there. It never was a problem to throw an impromptu meal together for ten or fifteen people and it meant that the "kids" got to provide fish or rabbits at short notice, which we could in those days. Of course with John having a car there was always the pictures or bowling alley and soccer trips in the winter.

Not only would these visitors travel many miles to visit Les and Beryl but they would do the same in reciprocation. I had only been in Australia for a short time when we took one such trip to the quaint little mountain township of Tumbarumba. A mere two hundred miles from Lanyon, we set out one Friday afternoon with just about everyone in the family in an old Peugeot with the doors that opened backwards and I have no idea how we all fitted, but we did. People that I corresponded with in England could not comprehend this logistic exercise as even the distances were foreign to them. But surely enough, at some time in the night we arrived at Uncle Jim and Aunty Thelma's house at Murrays Crossing in Tumbarumba.

There was always a huge amount of hugging and sloppy aunty type kisses followed by the compulsory cups of tea and gossip that could make or break reputations with the ferocity of a speeding train. I was always astounded how the bush telegraph could function so well in the days before our IT progress. But of course authentication was not always possible either and the gossip was as much a part of the entertainment as anything else. Added to all of this were the declarations about each other's children such as, "My, hasn't your Tricia grown up since we last saw her", or "And this must be young Robin, what do you think of Australia then?" But no time for an answer because the adults were unstoppable for the first hour of reunion.

Sleeping spaces were allocated and bags carried from the car. The local lads spoke sparingly and when they did it was amongst themselves, and I put this down to them feeling that their territory was being invaded and their routine changed out of their comfort zone. There were four boys and a girl in the Tumba family, with Judy the girl being the youngest and about the same age as Patricia. Judy and Patricia were very close and could have been sisters the way they related to each other. The boys were aged from about my age upwards and they all seemed to have their own cars and appeared to be a bit more worldly than me. That was more of an illusion rather than a fact and probably caused by being in their territory. The house was undergoing a lot of renovations which had been a long-term project and would take many years to complete yet. And so, when I awoke the next morning, I was quite surprised to find that on the other side of the bed there was no floor. Even greater was my surprise because that was the side that I got out on. Apart from a bit of bark off and an acute case of embarrassment, no major harm was done. Breakfast in the bush is the most important meal of the day and at Aunty Thelma's this was most evident with toast piled high and a plate the size of the car bonnet with bacon, eggs, chops, mushrooms, tomatoes, kidney, and lambs' fry. It was enough to "stick to your ribs" as Les would bellow in amongst his laughter.

After breakfast, Les took me for my first trip around Tumbarumba to show me all of the things that he was so obviously proud of. You can always tell a lot about places that hold a special place in people's lives with the enthusiasm that they have and the light in their eyes when they talk of the things that they had done there. Even the smallest details are cherished when talking of such places and Tumbarumba was, and I suspect still is, the most cherished place in Les Perrott's life. He showed me the house that he was brought up in and spoke of how determined his father was to perform all of those hard tasks with only one arm and places that he had been to and things that he did there.

There were creeks which were full of Rainbow and Brook Trout and foothills below the mountainous terrain that yielded the wild bush horses, and he was disappointed when we had to return to Thelma's house. He had one more surprise in store, however, and he set me up really well with our next visit to relatives.

I've been to Tumbarumba many times and lived there for ten years, and the place that we visited has changed very little in all that time. I am not sure who these relatives were or where they fitted into the big family tree but they were at best different. We pulled into a fairly standard driveway and up to what appeared to be a fairly standard house. The front had a full-length veranda and lined up along this veranda were the occupants. Not one smile, just all of these blank staring faces and the hairs on the back of my neck weren't just standing up, they were already running off down the road. Les sat in the car for some time as if reluctant to get out, which further concerned me because nothing in this world ever worried or frightened him. I cast my gaze along the line. There were two women nearest the front door, one obviously the mother and one I assumed to be a daughter. Both wore plain old dresses and were no doubt not strangers to hard work, which I found out to be the truth of the matter. The others were men from about mid-twenties to the one I presumed to be the father in his fifties, whose stare was the most intent and made more threatening with the stockwhip coiled around his forearm. The "boys" all wore jackets and heavy-duty trousers with cuffs and big boots and battered hats. One was idly scratching his scrotum, another spat on the garden bed, and the smallest one on the end of the veranda gently cuddled and stroked a pet rabbit. "Come on", Les bellowed, nearly sending me through the roof of the car, and with that he got out and headed for the veranda with that deep boisterous laugh of his echoing in my ears.

We were ushered into the kitchen and offered the compulsory cup of tea and slices of cake. The first observation was that the house had no floors, at least not wooden or concrete, they were just dirt. But the dirt shone like polished lino and was kept that way with constant sweeping and the walls were all cornflake packets that had been used as moulds for the mud bricks that were the walls of the house. The doors and internal beams and frames were hand-cut from local hardwood trees and each was meticulously finished. They had built the whole house themselves and they were ruled with an iron hand by the patriarchal figure. Les showed me the boundary fence and told me that one post was slightly out of alignment and the father had whipped the boys, made them pull the whole fence down and rebuild it. So, our visit to this household was a "fun" day for them.

Saturday night was party night and the smell of burnt offerings soon assailed the nostrils and the visits to the toilet tree became more frequent as the conversations turned to the resolving of all matters national and international. The older men spoke of heady days of breaking horses and rummy nights in the Tumba pub, the younger ones of cars and beery nights in the Tumba pub. And I took it all in and learned more about the Australian way of life.

The good old standby on the social calendar was the dance at the Tharwa Hall. Not exactly the sixties version of the Blue Light Disco but an event that no self-respecting country kid could miss out on. I couldn't dance to save my life but I looked the part as I did the Twist and the Shake and gave my best Buddy Holly impersonation. Patricia would get a bit protective at times and at that point I didn't understand why. Surely it was my responsibility to bring some joy and happiness to the lives of these fine folk. After all, I had seen the Beatles, and that made me an expert.

"I saw that," she'd say.

"What?" I would reply.

"You touched her."

"Of course I did, we're dancing."

"Now you're staring at her."

"No, I'm not."

SLAP. Yep, I just loved those dances at the old Tharwa Hall. We were to have our wedding reception there and I made her promise not to get agro if I danced with anyone female. "Of course I won't silly," but she had that smile in her eyes. I was going to tell you about the time I got caught snogging on the tennis courts but really it was far too violent for this forum.

It's off to the Cry Room for you two! In the mid-sixties, the picture theatre in Queanbeyan had one of those dudgeons for those silly enough to take a baby to the pictures. So why take a baby you ask! Patricia's baby sister Lorraine had been born and Beryl, in her infinite wisdom, thought that nights at the pictures would be so much more fun for us if we took the time to bond with the charming young bub. This of course was never a problem until Lorraine decided that she wanted a feed or just wanted to scream the house down. It was then that the ushers would shine their spotlights straight at us and say, "Sorry but you'll have to take bub to the Cry Room sir."

"She's not mine," I would protest. "It's her sister."

"Yes, of course sir, but I must insist because you're annoying the other patrons."

And so, it would be Pat and I pushing our way past another row of irate patrons and me hoping that Lorraine would spew on someone or produce one of those hugely offending smells that babies are so capable of. And all the while I would be protesting that she wasn't mine and all the while the old biddies making smart remarks about keeping it in my pants and you get what you deserve and stuff like that. For those who care, the seats in the cry room were hard and the room smelled like little baby waste products, and the speakers were terrible, and we usually just went home. I was glad that there was an alternative in the Drive-In-Theatre when we could go in really casual clothes and didn't get thrown in the room. But that's all I intend writing about drive-ins.

There were endless things for we young country kids to do and we made a lot of our own fun. And we didn't need a host of electronic equipment to do it.

CHAPTER SEVENTEEN

2789840 RECRUIT REED R.C.

Lanyon had been a wonderful time for the four or so years that I had been there before I came to the realisation that my tranquillity could be shattered by an Act of Parliament. Although it appeared to me to be remote, there was an ever-increasing chance that within a few months I could be conscripted and eventually end up on the battlefields of South Vietnam. I was in no way prepared for this and my natural reaction was to put it out of my mind and deal with it if it occurred. Cousin James must have also recognised the possibility that his recommendation of the good life may get me killed. I received a letter from him that winter, which in essence offered me the opportunity to return to England for the princely sum of $59.00 (one way) and all I needed to do was obtain my British passport.

It was for me the easiest decision of my life to date but there were others to consider and for once my decision would not be simply the selfish one. The fact that I considered myself to be at worst a fringe dweller in the Perrott family and had a great respect for John and his solidness and that I loved the lifestyle all would suggest that to stay was the obvious choice. Of course there were now other reasons to stay and I had given them a lot of thought, which surprised me. All of the decisions in my life so far were either made for me or they were impulsive and based on very little rationale. Here at Lanyon, I had actually started to map out something of a career path and a plan into the future.

Shortly after arriving in Australia and settled to the lifestyle, I had started a correspondence course with Stotts and had nearly completed the modules of Soil Management, Husbandry, and Wool Production. Although I was addicted to the life of stockman, I had also realised that as a long-term prospect the days of glamour in the saddle were numbered. I could already see a deterioration in Les's physical self, which had been brought about by many years of bouncing around in a saddle and the hard manual work of a station hand. And so I had made the decision that after these modules were finished I would investigate doing a Diploma in Soil Management and/or Pasture Improvement and try for a job with a government department, something like the CSIRO. I had kept this fairly close to the chest, for fear of failure I suppose but also because the plan included a long-term relationship with Patricia. I could see it in my head, good job, lots of children, house in the burbs, and this as much as anything was affecting any decision about returning to the UK. The possibility that I might get killed had not even been a consideration.

I wrote to James and told him that I thought that it was a remote likelihood that I would be conscripted and that I would risk all of the bad things for the more satisfying long-term prospects. Besides which I didn't want to go back to England.

I then settled back to more of the good life until one day I got this lovely little note from someone of authority asking me to pop over to the Canberra Community Hospital on a given date where I would be medically assessed for suitability to become a National Serviceman. The prospect of this all being a reality was a little bit closer but still it had not really dawned that it could happen. I spoke to many nashos during my Army life and it is surprising the number who, until getting on the bus, didn't really grasp the fact that they were cannon fodder for a government desperate to please Uncle Sam.

On the appointed day, I found myself sitting in a large waiting room in the hospital clad only in my boxers with a folder of papers in one hand and a bottle of urine in the other. This was so easy for me because I was raised to be lined up and told what to do. There was the usual nervous bravado in the group as "expert" knowledge was bandied around on how to fail our medical. Swallow chewing gum or silver paper just before the X-ray, drink lots of orange juice to disrupt the urine sample, swear that you have distant relos with terrible but largely unknown mental disorders and tell them that you are a chronic sleepwalker and snorer. We must have thought that these doctors were the idiots, but I don't know of any failures at the medical.

The most fascinating part of the procedure was a psychological test which was a written test with all sorts of what I presumed to be trick questions. You know the type of thing, if this cog turns anticlockwise in this series of cogs, then which way will that one turn, Jonny has six apples, how many did he steal, and if the smoke on the train was blowing south and the, and so forth. We all had to be present and do the test at the same time and so as we finished the other parts of the medical, we were ushered into a classroom and instructed to sit, be quiet, and don't touch anything until told to do so. All of this by a real soldier who identified himself as being from a Psych Unit. I was amazed that they would have such a thing let alone letting them out for the day.

I did everything that I could to get all of the questions wrong, and though I realised it was somewhat childish, I saw it as the last defiant gesture and felt that I had bucked the system in some small way. My AAB83 Record of Service, which I still have, says that I have a psych rating of SG1 and am capable of being trained to a highly skilled level in most clerical and mechanical postings in the Army. How was anyone to fail the medical?

After the medical, we all went back to our diverse lives and once again, I honestly forgot about the possibility of conscription. Then, like a bolt from the blue, I got the serious letter which brought my world crashing down and for one small moment I wished that I'd taken the trip to England. No "Dear Mr Reed", this time, no way. It was "you have been selected" and lots of other "you are to"s and "you are not to"s. The bottom line was that on first May 1968 I was to be at the Tourist Bureau in Civic Centre where a bus would convey me to the 1st Recruit Training Battalion (lRTB) at Wagga Wagga to commence two years of National Service. For months, this day had been a definite possibility and although I had refused to accept that possibility up until now, it came as an absolute body blow to now realise that I was to be sent to Vietnam and might very well be killed.

And so on the appointed day, Les and Beryl took me to Canberra where we all shook hands, hugged and stuff, and all of these short haired civvies were herded onto the bus by a group of green-clad sheepdogs who barked out orders that we didn't understand nor cared to. Pat and I cuddled for too long for one sheepdog and I think it was just as well that I couldn't understand him or it may have got nasty about then. Names were called out and answered as we each boarded the bus, a late arrival was yelled at, and one who didn't turn up at all had his parentage and manhood questioned and eventually we were all on board and the bus was off to Wagga Wagga. The process of cloning had started, and if the Army is good at anything, it is churning out little green blocks that fit into other green blocks that go to make up the big green block called the Army.

The transition from a diverse and uncoordinated rabble that marched into lRTB to the coordinated well-drilled platoon of soldiers that marched out took about eight weeks and remains one of the wonders of the world to me. I could not begin to detail those eight weeks because they are contained in volumes of military documents that cannot be described any further. There are some aspects of that training, however, that must be retold.

Live firing ranges were the most controlled of military activities in that time, and even still, the thought of some bank clerk with an SLR and John Wayne Syndrome can wake me at night in a cold sweat. But it wasn't just rifles that worried me, for we had to throw live grenades as well. Can you imagine the sweaty palms at our first live grenade practice? We were marched to an area some distance from the main body of the camp to an area that looked like a big toilet block with a tower at the rear, and we lined up in three ranks behind ground sheets with grenades on them. We had, of course, done some training on the grenade and touched them before, but these ones looked real. With an instructor at every position, we were again run through the safety precautions and we got to strip what turned out to be dummy ones on the groundsheets. The next question had me puzzled at first and then puzzlement turned into sweaty palms again. How many left-handers are there? A strange request I thought but had become used to strange requests, and so I indicated my molly dookedness only to be frowned upon because when it came to throwing grenades lefties were the equivalent to lepers at a fitness centre. The potential for body parts to fly through the air was the same. If you have never thrown a grenade, then I cannot begin to tell you how difficult it is for left-handers. For those unfortunates, the grenade is upside down and the pin pointing in the wrong direction and worse is that the clip doesn't fit snugly in the palm as it does for right-handers. I was all of the things that you don't want to be at the grenade range and I was the first one in the bunker. Never has a grenade been held so tightly or thrown as far as mine was and then afterwards when I was lying in the shade and everyone else was experiencing the terror, I was so blasé.

The rifle range was equally scary because of the John Wayne Syndrome. If you think about it you will know what I mean. The man next to you has no idea about the potential of the piece of metal and wood in his care and despite all of the safety training, I've seen people turning around on the firing mound with their rifle pointing everywhere. It does have its lighter moments however, and the simplest of body functions can lighten up most situations.

There are usually three rounds fired first as sighting rounds to give the shooter an opportunity to know how their rifle is shooting and to get used to finding the sight picture. Most recruits don't even know what a sight picture is, but it is good practice for real shoots later on. To ensure that the maximum safety is achieved, firing details are kept to as small a number as possible, so that each recruit has an instructor with him.

Fine, so far. The officer in charge has a megaphone to issue instructions and orders and would say something like "With a three-round magazine, LOAD," at which time a magazine is placed on the rifle. "READY," and the rifle is cocked with safety catch applied and then, "One sighting round in your own time, GO ON." At this time, you fire one round at the target. He would then say, "Targets down, patch out." Same for the second and third rounds so that each time you could see where, or indeed if, you hit the target. After the command GO ON there is always a huge silent pause. Rifles are cocked with safety catches off and people are desperately trying to get the perfect sight picture. At this point on the first detail of the first shoot of 9 Platoon, one of the firing details, did the loudest, most vulgar sounding fart that Kapooka has ever experienced. This was one that had movie goers rolling in the aisles and fathers wait for years of finger pulling to achieve. The result here was for six recruits to start mock humping the ground with laughter while instructors tried bellowing instructions through their laughter, and the officer tried to get the safety catches applied whilst laughing into his megaphone, and eventually through controlled chaos some semblance of normality was resumed. And the officer calmly through his megaphone said, "Targets down, patch out, fall out the officers," and the shoot progressed again.

Everything in the Army is done in lines and by the numbers. To get our inoculations, we would line up alphabetically, shirts off and move past the medics getting jabs to the left, then right then left again until you were outside, shirt on and lined up again. It was so predictable and the only variations were the words that the instructors used as impact statements. Our sergeant never swore at his recruits but always achieved the desired impact with tact and timing. I remember he would stare at his victim until the poor recruit would eventually look back at him and he had him. Without blinking, he would point at his victim and say, "Don't stare at me son, I'm married." If he ever saw anyone with their arms folded, he would call them out of the ranks and ask them, "Only pregnant women and homosexuals fold their arms, are you pregnant recruit?" Others were not so careful with their responses to recruits' stuff-ups and would be at times foul-mouthed and obnoxious with such retorts as, "I'll pull your foreskins over your heads and make you look like red-back spiders," or "Feet shoulder width apart, your guts won't drop out."

And so, after about eight weeks my transition from Mr Robin Clive Reed, civilian stockman, to 2789840 Private Reed R.C. soldier in progress was complete.

CHAPTER EIGHTEEN

MR AND MRS REED

As the Pass Out Parade faded into the distance and I prepared to leave Kapooka for my first posting to an Infantry Battalion at Liverpool near Sydney and more training, my brave fiancé and her parents were discussing, quite energetically, the merits of she and I becoming married.

Pat and I had no doubt that it was a logical follow on in our lives and our relationship because we were in love. I had not simply dodged talking with Les and Beryl and felt bad that Pat would have to do this alone, but we had only enough time to talk to each other before the Army in its wisdom decided that I should be packed and ready to move in only minutes after we marched off the parade ground. We had discussed the real possibility of me not returning from Vietnam and that would mean that we would have had no life together to enjoy the simplest of things that married couples enjoy. We weren't considering the close and tender things but wanted to share the menial day-to-day things like eating dinner, talking about each other's day, doing the dishes, and cuddling up to a night of TV.

Les and Beryl had everything and everyone on their side and should have won the discussion. Our marriage would be a disaster, we had no money, we had no furniture or anywhere to live, and we were just plain and simple too young and needed their approval. I was going to a far-off country to fight a dirty war, and what if she were to fall pregnant and I didn't come back? How could I contemplate doing these things to the girl that I was supposed to love and who would raise a child from our union? No! was the emphatic and final answer; it was not going to happen. Pat played the trump card and told her parents that she would go to Sydney anyway and if she fell pregnant, so be it, but we would spend our time together. A ridiculous argument indeed and one which would never have happened but it won the day for her; they agreed and 3rd August 1968 was the set date. She rang my new unit and had the message passed on to me.

After my initial elation on hearing the news, I have to be absolutely honest and say that I almost immediately started to think that it was the wrong thing to do. There were so many negatives. I was about to embark on a roller coaster ride in the Army that could end in any number of ways, some of which didn't bear thinking about, we didn't have anywhere to live and no money or furniture. I would be away on exercises for most of the time before Vietnam and how could I subject someone that I loved to that sort of a beginning to our married life? Had I had the opportunity to talk to Pat face-to-face I would have tried to call the marriage off. Thankfully, I didn't get that opportunity because by the next day we had started Corps training and I didn't get the chance to talk to anybody. The moment I got Pat's message I spoke to my Sergeant and surprisingly he didn't say much other than to consult some training programme and confirm that my getting married fitted in with the Army's' schedule and he would arrange for my pay, train ticket, and leave pass to be ready on 1st August and that I would be required back for an exercise on the 5th of August. From then until the first I was full on training and true to its word, I was back at 5RAR lines by lunch time on the first.

I was about to learn several things about life in the army, none of which was to endear me to it or the people who ran it. As soon as I got back, I raced to the rooms and showered, changed, packed my bag and presented to the orderly room. "I've come for my ticket and pay," says I. "What are you talking about," says the clerk in front of me. I've seen that look many times since then. It is the totally blank look that is generally followed by the best buck-passing exercise known to mankind and the frustration had just started. I sat and waited and about an hour later someone produced a Leave Pass. "What about my pay?" I asked. "We are working on that now," was the stern reply, as if I was some parasite trying to suck the system dry. By now it was late afternoon and then miraculously my pay arrived and I duly signed for it. "What about my ticket?" says I. By now the orderly room was closing for the day and the duty staff were arriving and my chance of getting a ticket on anything that day had disappeared. "Looks like you will have to thumb it," was the best advice that I was going to get that day. I would have waited and travelled on the Friday but I had so much to do and only one day to do it in. I had a suit to fit, a ring to buy, practices to walk through and let's not forget the "buck's party". And so, at about five o'clock in the afternoon on a wintry Thursday, I started off from Liverpool bound for Lanyon with my thumb pointing ever southwards.

Hitchhiking has never been my preferred method of travel and on the old Hume Highway in the dark of a winter's night it became even less desirable than my recent training. It took until three in the morning for me to finally walk the last ten miles and fall in the door of Les and Beryl's house at Lanyon. I was exhausted and frozen to the bone and wanted to fall onto anything comfortable and fall asleep, but this was not going to happen as everyone was talking at the same time and Pat was crying and "Why didn't you ring?", "How many people stopped for you?", "How about a nice cup of tea?", "Are you hungry?", and a million other questions. "Please!" I was saying, "I'm tired and cold and I need to sleep for a little while." My army training had no doubt helped my journey and made me lighter and fitter. Sleep must have just overtaken everything else because I remember waking up on Friday with Pat sitting on the end of the bed. She said, "Time to get up sleepy, we have a big day ahead." All my attempts to get her to join me failed so I got up and got ready for the big day ahead. Friday was a blur but I remember trying on my suit and the look of joy on Pat's face when we agreed on the ring. There were discussions with the Reverend Crossley and some practicing and finally all of the arrangements were complete and we were back at Lanyon and I was getting ready for the buck's party. Four weeks of intensive Infantry training, ten hours of hitchhiking, all day shopping and trying on clothes, and now I was to be escorted around Queanbeyan in an almighty pub crawl.

"Please John, don't let the bastards do anything stupid tonight or Vietnam may seem the lesser of two evils when Pat gets to me."

"Don't worry," he said, but I did.

There are, for me, five stages of pissed-ness. The first stage was reached fairly quickly when output seems to be greater than intake and trips to the dunny are frequent. And so intake slows and the first of the coordination stages kicks in. During this stage I'm getting louder but am still coherent and need some support from the edge of the bar or table. Stage three is when I think that I'm coherent but am really talking loudly and in brail, find focusing difficult and develop the drunkard sway. This stage can last for quite some time but once it is reached, the next stages are almost unstoppable. I have stopped at stage three and found that sleep will not come and the rotating room syndrome has developed with a similarity to rides at Luna Park. You must keep your eyes open but you have to sleep which is impossible and this leads to an intimacy with the white porcelain bowl. This night I pushed on regardless to stage four which requires every shred of willpower to concentrate on even the smallest things. The broad knowledge of your surroundings has gone and all of your focus and energies are concentrated on the area within a space no bigger than an average-sized broom closet. I have known people in this state who have thought they needed to pee and have done so in someone's front lounge room because they couldn't focus any further than that. I am able to change that point of focus and as such I managed to reach the dunny door almost unaided. I say almost unaided because, evidently, I did bounce off a few irate customers and walls on my way there. Having navigated successfully to the toilet, I immediately went to stage five and crumpled in a pathetic, comatose heap on the floor and remained there. The barman, who I never thanked, enquired of my chaperones if they were of my acquaintance and after all had denied me, he propped me up against the wall and said, "Just remember to take him home with you when you leave," and they did.

For some reason I was not allowed back to Les's house, although my beloved was in no danger of premature molestation. Instead, John and I were ferried to a friend's house at Cuppacumbalong near Tharwa. Mr and Mrs Jones were really nice people and Laurie was one of my drinking partners that night. Mrs Jones summed up my situation very quickly and quite rightly decided that they should clean me up a bit. A high-pressure hose would have been the most appropriate but being a lady of fine country stock, she decided that the personal touch of female brutality would be the best solution. Having now evacuated the contents of my stomach at various venues between Queanbeyan and Tharwa, stage five had turned into a complete lack of coordination and the ability to talk. Evidently, I did manage an occasional "ow" and "argh" during the de-robing process, which was caused by a very sensitive piece of skin being entrapped in the fly mechanism of my trousers. Mrs Jones never mentioned the problem except for a passing comment the next morning when she said, "Hope I didn't ruin the little fella's night out."

"It's only a flesh wound," I bravely conceded.

Somehow, I managed to be presentable on Saturday the third of August 1968 and duly stood in the small Tharwa church complete with organ music provided by a local lady who performed with gusto, and the sun beaming in narrow shafts through the bullet holes from some misguided juveniles' pea rifles. Even our small country wedding attracted more people than the church could accommodate, and Pat had to push her way through the crowds just to get in the front door. I should mention that ours was the first wedding in the Tharwa church in eighty years and the next was that of the charming Penny Hackforth Jones. I believe that it is now quite "trendy" to use the quaint facility.

The ceremony was exactly what Pat had hoped for and she was as beautiful on that day as she has been every day since. Everyone did those things that we had practiced, and we paraded out of the church as Mr and Mrs Reed into a chilly August afternoon, whilst the congregation took box brownies and Kodak photos, and the old biddies tittered behind their hands asking each other if we would be taking our baby with us and assuring each other that it will never last. What would we know about being man and wife; we were still babies ourselves. The baby that they referred to was Pat's sister Lorraine who is only a couple of years older than our daughter Margaret and had on many occasions been our unsuspecting chaperone at the movies. We stood outside the Tharwa church until Uncle Digger's little white Toyota ferried us up the four hundred metres to the village hall for the reception. The family had done a wonderful transformation from the drab old dancehall that I was used to into a profusion of balloons and streamers with snow-white rolls of white paper on the tables and all the places set and marked with a name. For those of you who have experienced the reception held in a small country town, not unlike the "Dimboola Wedding", this scene would bring back wonderful memories of times that didn't need expensive reception centres and a Planner with a gourmet three-course feast. This was an earthy gathering of people who would bring a plate of food and dance and enjoy themselves. A function when the speeches were full of basic language which came from the heart and with sincerity. It was a reception that I will never forget, not just because it was for mine and Pat's marriage but because it was indicative of my life on Lanyon Station with people who told it as it was and enjoyed life that was at times hard but always fulfilling. We ate, danced, drank, and made merry until the clock struck time for us to race away for a night of debauchery, even with my injured appendage. We drove back to Lanyon and picked up our suitcase and headed off for our honeymoon.

I say honeymoon but in fact it was just a night in a motel in Queanbeyan because the army had allowed all the time it was going to and I had to be back in Liverpool for first parade on

Monday morning. However, I can assure everyone that despite the injury we had a most pleasant evening. Sunday morning and we were back at Lanyon bright and early. Les met me at the door and in his booming voice said, "Don't bring her back here, I gave her away yesterday." This was followed by his equally booming laughter. Les and Beryl took us to Liverpool that day and we moved into an on-site caravan at Milperra with the few possessions that we had, shook hands and hugged and watched as our parents drove off into the sunset. This was it; in the space of four days, we had gone from two young kids with starry eyes and a belief in ourselves to a married couple living in a caravan park in Milperra with barely enough of anything to start our life together. It's an old adage that love will see you through, but we still had to eat and pay the bills and get to work and we hadn't really worked any of these things out yet.

CHAPTER NINETEEN

A BAGGY GREEN HUSBAND

Bright and early on Monday morning I kissed my new bride goodbye and started the walk to Holsworthy. In my green skin it was not difficult to get a ride to the barracks and I found myself in the room and bedspace allocated to me in more than enough time for first parade. There was even enough time to have some breakfast in the OR's mess. It was amazing how when I entered the Battalion area I was immediately changed back into a soldier, almost as if the previous four days had happened to someone else. The "system" was to turn this day into one which finally taught me that as a married National Serviceman I had as many rights and entitlements as, and would be treated the same as, any piece of equipment held in the Quartermaster's store. That is all we were, a piece of army property to use as the army saw fit. A mate of mine once said, "we are only cannon fodder," and I was to learn very quickly how true that was.

During my Corps training the sergeant in charge of us had told me of wondrous things that would be available to me once I was married. A married rate of pay and a married quarter for us to live in within the army village. A place where Pat would have support from the Community Services people and army wives to guide her through the coming traumatic times when I would be in Vietnam. The rental would be low, there would be free medical for me and membership to the Army Health Scheme for Pat. With all this in mind, I requested an interview with my Platoon Commander who was a Corps of Signals Captain and at that time I believed he would have mine and Pat's best interests at heart. During the interview he slowly but surely informed me that there would be no married quarter for us and no special rate of pay and no access to anything that he could see so, "Get back out on parade and stop whingeing like a big sook." My relationship with the good Captain Laurie Ganter began a downward spiral that did not improve right up until the time that he was moved out of the Battalion for whatever the reason. Shortly after this interview, the wives were invited to a function for the Platoon to get to know each other and to allow some good PR for the green machine, and perhaps gloss over the forthcoming months in that sort of "Policing type of thing" in Vietnam. Captain Ganter was privileged to talk to Pat and he asked her what she thought of the army in general and the prospect of Vietnam in particular. Not yet being aware of the protocols that were expected of her she told the truth and amid the stares of all of those around us I felt immensely proud of her but knew that there would be repercussions. The allocations within the Platoon followed soon after and my turn to stand at attention in front of the OC came. "What would you like to do in the Platoon structure?" asked my fearless leader as he moved toy tanks and trucks around on his desktop. "I would like to be in the Line Section," said I whilst still maintaining my best "at attention" pose. "Well, you are not, in fact you are going to be a radio operator," he snapped at me. And that was the end of the allocation interview.

For the rest of August and then through September, October, November, and into December I spent only short periods in our caravan and more time either in barracks or away on exercises. My other homes included the Holsworthy Close Training Area,

O'Hares Creek, Tianjara, Tin Can Bay, Jungle Training Centre at Canungra and any other nasty little area that the army could find to make mine and the rest of the battalion's lives as miserable as possible. I learned more in those few months to make me despise the army and all that it stood for than in the last eighteen years of my military service. During all of this time, Pat was a tower of strength and I cannot remember any occasion that she put pressure on me for not being home but rather she was totally supportive of our lifestyle and just got on and made the best of the short periods we had together. In fact, I can only remember one disagreement that we had, and that was over my parade greens. For those who know anything about army life you would appreciate the meticulous care taken over parade equipment. Brass was shining brightly, boots were spit-polished to the point where you could see your reflection in them, and your uniform was starched and pressed into almost razor-sharp creases. We had a particularly important parade for which even the best efforts previously were to be improved on. I spent hours on my belt, rifle sling, magazine, and boots, and Pat spent hours on starching and pressing my greens. The day arrived and I went to take all of this gear into barracks and almost fainted when I looked at the greens and they were stiff as a board and streaked with white from being immersed in the starch solution. I was dead, probably to be beheaded at the very least but there was nothing I could do to get out of being on parade. Unfortunately, I reflected my anguish to Pat and was not as diplomatic as I should have been. To her they were simply silly clothes that grown men tried to look impressive in, so what if there were a few starchy streaks in them? Try as I might, I could not convey to her the disaster that was about to occur when I paraded in front of the Battalion RSM dressed in those greens. Two things were the direct outcome of this saga, firstly, Pat did not ever again do my parade clothing, and secondly, I received an absolute bollocking from my Company Sergeant Major and was allocated the task of cleaning the SAL block for the next fortnight. SAL standing for shower and latrine.

The training was very intense and I was learning the little ways that soldiers use to try and get out of doing things. I have to admit that I never used the RAP or some feigned illness or domestic emergency to stay back in barracks. The only time I tried was only a joke when I asked Jock, our Platoon Sergeant, if I could be excused because my wife was pregnant.

"She's not pregnant Reedy."

"Yes, she is Jock," I protested.

"When did this happen?" he asked.

"About four hours ago." I giggled and was promptly given a playful swipe from Jock that knocked me off the wooden seats along the truck. Jock was a Scot and built like a bear who loved Rugby Union, drinking and his wife Betty. I was forming friendships in the army, some of which could have lasted for a lifetime if I or they could have forced ourselves to make the effort after Vietnam or postings away from each other. I suppose it happens in every walk of life that people grow out of friendships and develop new interests and priorities. In years to come I was to see most of them one final time at the Welcome Home march in Sydney. I think of them from time to time and hope that they think of me too.

Before I embarked for Vietnam, Pat ran into some old friends of ours from Lanyon and they invited us to their house for dinner. Alan and Estelle and their children lived at Casula on a small poultry farm that produced hundreds of dozens of eggs, and Alan had many other jobs such as Electrolux salesman, Swipe Consultant, and Insurance Salesman. He liked to think of himself as some sort of entrepreneur and I have to be honest he could talk under water with a mouth full of marbles. They invited us to stay with them for the remainder of the time that we were in Sydney and so we moved out of the caravan and onto the chook farm. It was one of those agreements that was not formalised in writing but rather a shake of the hand whereby Pat and I helped out with the gathering and cleaning of eggs and in return we had our own bedroom and shared the food and general domestic duties. Pat worked hard with Estelle around the chook farm and Alan and I went off to work each day. On weekends I cleaned out under the cages and did the heavier work in the sheds for which I had the use of an old motorbike to go to work on. It all worked reasonably well and helped immensely with filling in a gap with our accommodation requirements and gave Pat a far more secure place to be while I was away on exercises. There was another fringe benefit which allowed us to go to the movies every night. Alan and Estelle lived right next door to the Casula Drive-In Theatre and our bedroom looked straight at the big screen. On the warm summer nights, we could open our window and lay back in bed and watch the movies and hear the sound perfectly. This was a long time before I became half deaf, and in those days, I could stay awake right through the full Saturday night programme.

Pat and I enjoyed married life and managed to fit in enough time together to go on picnics, walks, laze around on the riverbanks, and do our little bit of shopping, and although the time was fast approaching for me to leave for at least twelve months we didn't dwell on it but rather simply enjoyed being Mr and Mrs from day to day and hoping that time could stand still forever. I got some Pre-Embarkation Leave and we spent that with Les and Beryl and the family, and then I was being loaded onto HMAS Sydney and waving goodbye to everyone, and in particular, my pregnant wife.

There is that period in my life that I have refused to talk about and even refused to acknowledge that it existed, but to make this a complete account of my life I must include it in this book and it is with great difficulty that I do so. Those closest to me will be aware of some of this for the first time and I hope they can forgive me for not sharing it with them before I do so with the rest of the people who read this. It is the most wasted and fruitless period of my life and is of course the period from February 1969 to March 1970 in what was then South Vietnam. This is about the tenth time that this chapter has been attempted and this time it will simply be, do it and move on, because no number of attempts will satisfy me other than to not include it at all, which would be like tearing out some pages from a good story and being dishonest to you, the reader.

I never really understood the reasons for my being told to be in the Army and train to go to Vietnam. People had talked of the Communist Threat and the need to halt the effects and possible results of the "Domino Theory", but there was nothing real or tangible in my life to support what they said. No foreign force was trying to take over Lanyon Station and I hadn't seen the yellow hordes ravaging Queanbeyan or Canberra other than the cranky operator of the odd Chinese Restaurant. LBJ's visit to Lanyon had been disruptive to my daily routine and now it was to change my life forever. Surely the most powerful people in the world would not send me off to help in a war unless there was some real, if underlying, reason. I have recently read an interesting book called "Curveball" and I can now believe that these most powerful of people can and do make the most devastating and incorrect decisions, and they can be purely driven by the need to appease the really powerful people. Conscription was a popular policy with the voting public in the early days of the Vietnam conflict, but by 1969 the tide was turning fast and the government of the day appeared to distance itself from that which they had earlier so enthusiastically endorsed.

And so, I found myself on the flight deck of HMAS Sydney watching the lights of Vung Tau creep ever closer during my picquet and thinking, "What the fuck am I doing here?" The first thing that I noticed was the smell of what I thought was something unique to this place but have since found that many Asian places have a similar smell. This was followed by the sight of such poverty and filth which seemed to be everywhere in this port town. To say that I thought that all of Vietnam was like this is not true because I now know that the village people in that country are as clean as their situation allows and they are generally just hardworking people who could not understand any more than I why their country should be torn apart by war. The difference between me and them was that I hoped to be leaving as soon as my tour was over.

I see no reason to legitimise my time with a blow-by-blow description of the time that I spent "in country" and it will suffice to say that I was no hero or even close to it. I went through the mechanics of being a soldier and existed on a day-to-day basis until it was time to once again stand on the flight deck of HMAS Sydney and watch Vung Tau fading into the distance and thinking, "Thank fuck that's over." No "Long Tan, Coral or Balmoral" for me, no fighting out of deadly "horseshoe" bunker systems but rather the need to simply be there at the end of each day so that I could write another letter to my wife and thereby maintain the thread with the reality of getting home again.

There was one highlight in 1969 and that was the receipt of a telegram from Beryl which read, "DAUGHTER BORN STOP BOTH MOTHER AND DAUGHTER DOING WELL STOP." I knew then that there was a part of me that was going to survive in this world no matter what my fate was to be. We were in Nui Dat at the time and with two mates I celebrated for three days and remember nothing except I didn't write during the binge. I took my R&R in Australia and the feeling that I had when holding Margaret for the first time is something that I felt in the pit of my stomach and I nearly said I'm not going back there. How could I return to that foul place after holding my baby girl and being reunited with my wife? But on the plane, I got and returned and saw out the rest of my time. Until you have known the expression 364 and a wakey for its reality then you cannot understand the depth of its meaning. For those who are expecting a list of gory details then I am sorry for I have none to tell you. Yes, I've seen what an exit wound looks like from a 7.62mm round, and seen the blank look of the dead, and I've listened to the trees being pruned, but I was lucky enough not to have walked into a bunker system or had to tippy toe over a mined LZ. And I've listened to the battalion radio net to CONTACT REPORTS, SITREPS, NOTICAS and FATACAS and heard them notify that one of my fellow recruits from Kapooka would not be going home alive. And if you think that this was not enough then I feel sorry for you and perhaps you should talk to the real heroes who have experienced things far worse than I did, but I doubt that they would talk to you just to satisfy some morbid curiosity.

Of all the veterans that I have spoken to, none of them have been seeking sympathy but rather understanding and support and thankfully forty plus years later there is now a lot more support than immediately after the event. Vietnam was bad enough but the euphoria of returning with the battalion and the reception that we got completely destroyed my faith in our fellow Australians. After the unbelievable joy of holding my wife and daughter at Garden Island, the battalion marched through some of the streets of Sydney. I don't remember the route and it is really irrelevant, but I do remember that there weren't as many people as I'd expected, but that didn't matter. Many of the people waved their little flags and cheered with "Good onya digger", and "Welcome home fellas." But there were hundreds who jeered and called us baby killers and women rapers. They spat at us and threw rotten vegetation and even tipped their pisspots out from balconies. It wasn't just these morons that made me feel dirty and guilty but also the thought that we had been conned by governments who to maintain good relations with Uncle Sam had allowed young men to be killed and maimed. And even worse is the knowledge that Uncle Sam couldn't give a shit about Australia and used us to legitimise their actions. Twenty-five had died and over two hundred wounded in our battalion alone, and for no good reason at all.

After the parade we were dismissed and were given time to clear our accrued leave days. Margaret had measles and Les and Beryl took her back to Bungendore where they were living at the time. Pat and I went to visit an aunty and uncle in Hornsby and her cousins started with the questions as soon as we got in the door. "Did you, how many, what's it like, etc?" Luckily these relos were all Sally's and Aunty Kath took pity on me and asked us to go to the butcher's shop for some meat for dinner. I relate this to emphasise just how screwed up I was, for when we stood in the butcher's someone asked me if I had just got back from Vietnam on the Sydney. I looked them in the eye and said, "No mate," and then burst out crying for no good reason at all. This was supposed to one of the most relieved and happy days of my life and I'm standing there bawling. I thought that one of these Padre hours that we used to have would perhaps help with this confusion, but there were none and nobody ever sat us down and explained why we felt this way and how to become part of our daily lives in Australia. That I tried to strangle my wife on two occasions in my sleep and was irritable and short-tempered didn't seem to be anything but normal. Like I have said, there were others who had experienced far worse than I who must have been so disturbed that they would sink into their own worlds and shun society.

After an overnight stay with Kath and Neville, Pat and I booked into a motel and spent the next three days locked behind closed doors and caught up with some lost time. It was one reality that I could cling to when we were on our own with no one else to talk to.

It wasn't just the idiots who were taking the now popular line of berating Vietnam survivors but I found opposition in the strangest of places. My first night in Queanbeyan, which is where Pat had lived during my tour, was spent, by invitation, at the RSL Bowling Club. Again, I wanted to talk of normal things like football, politics, sex, or even the local gossip, but instead it was, "Did you, how many, what was it?" and so forth. I eventually was collared by an old, World War Two veteran, and thought at last I could get away from all this rubbish, but instead he accused me of grandstanding and that after all, I hadn't been in a real war like they were in. I couldn't believe what I was hearing so I just got well and truly pissed and was thankful when they got sick of me and sent us home in a taxi. For many years after, the only reason that I went into any RSL Club was to gamble and get as pissed as I could.

Many Nashos settled back into civvy street whilst others crawled and slid into things that were never the same as they left them. Others, like me, took the easy option and signed on in the Army. I figured there was nothing that they could do to me that hadn't already happened. I haven't regretted staying in, but often wonder how it would have turned out if we had opted to return to civvy street. Besides, I had a wife and daughter to look after and still hoped for a married quarter. Not many people had much time for the wives and families of soldiers in Vietnam. As I have mentioned, Pat moved to Queanbeyan and lived with her brother, uncle, and our good friend John Hamilton. Just before Margaret was born, the local Padre visited for the first and only time. Pat had believed that they only visited with grave news and she almost passed out and then became hysterical when she saw him. The labour with Margaret was long and extremely painful, lasting nearly three days. The staff at the Queanbeyan Hospital had decided that she was an unmarried girl who had played up with a soldier before he left and they treated her terribly. "Serves you right," they would say, and "You deserve everything you get for being such a little trollop!" Apart from family she got no help at all, which highlights just how lowly National Servicemen were thought of.

At the end of my leave, we went back to Sydney and found a flat in Carboni Street in Liverpool, and I went back to the battalion lines ready to resume being a peacetime solider.

CHAPTER TWENTY

TOWARDS THE END OF INFANTRY

There was something entirely different about the training that I was doing now to that of fifteen months ago. I suppose there would not have been much point in training to fight a war in SE Asia, therefore, the emphasis was on becoming qualified for promotions, expanding the signals skills and a strange thing called adventure training. Part of that adventure training involved things that they called "Fun Runs" which always seemed to be a contradiction of terms.

Peacetime Infantry life is a bit like wearing a raincoat during a drought. It looks pretty but doesn't serve a lot of purpose and eventually you will get tired of it and want something different. I had just put the raincoat on.

I should mention here that the Army had not improved its administrative functions very much and I suddenly became even more of an embarrassment to it. Soon after my return to barracks, the period of National Service expired and I signed on in the Regular Army for a period of three years, or so I thought. I should also explain the Army pay system at that time for those not enlightened amongst you. Someone in the big system had recognised the need for married soldiers to allocate part of their pay to a bank account so that the wives would not be left with no money if the soldiers decided to go to the RSL or Harold Park on the payday and miscalculate the amount of money they spent.

Consequently, I allocated the majority of my pay to our joint account, engaged for three years and applied for a Married Quarter. My specialist training then commenced at Ingleburn with attendance at a Signals NCO and Officer course. To my horror, when I marched into the course, I found that it was full of captains, lieutenants, warrant officers, and sergeants, and Lance Corporal Bob Reed. This is relevant to the administrative function only because it meant that I was away from home, again, and my Married Quarter Application was now "in the system" and it had reached SNAFU stage. Situation normal all fucked up.

Not being aware of this, I diligently applied myself to doing well in the training and for six weeks spent most of my time studying and passing tests. I also didn't know that the Army outside of 5RAR had assumed that I had been discharged at the end of my National Service and therefore I no longer existed. The good news is that I not only passed the course but topped it, to the disgust of all of those officers and senior NCOs. Back to the Battalion and asked about a Married Quarter and received that blank look that had been there after Pat and I were married.

"You're not entitled," I was eventually told, "Because you were married whilst in the same unit as now and you are a National Serviceman."

"Only right on one account," I corrected the Corporal. "I am now a regular soldier for three years."

That confused look slowly spread over his face and I got that sinking feeling in the pit of my stomach. Without another word, he took off down the corridor and came back with an officer that I didn't know but assumed was the Admin Officer or Platoon Commander.

"What seems to be the problem Corporal?" he asked as if I had all the answers rather than all of the questions.

I spent the next ten minutes explaining my situation to him, and after consulting with my Record of Service, he concluded with some flourish that, "There seems to be a bit of a problem here Corp." You know that it has gone horribly wrong when they start being nice. You also know that it's going to be a long, drawn-out process when they say, "Leave it with me and I'll try and sort it out." The days turned into weeks and more weeks and I did my promotion subjects for Corporal and then Sergeant and there was no further action on anything.

Life in the flat at Carboni St was great. There were four flats and three were occupied by soldiers, with the fourth being the owners. Pat and I lived on the upper level opposite the owner, and the downstairs ones by a Sapper and his wife and little girl, and a Transport Private and his wife. If I was home on Saturday mornings then the owner, a lovely old Italian chap, would invite us in for a taste of his brother's homemade red wine. I didn't like to be rude, and on many occasions, Saturday became a total write-off because he served his wine in schooner glasses and after one of them, I was wasted. But it maintained good relations with him and apart from Saturday we would rarely see him. The Sapper and his wife and daughter Kim became very good friends with Pat and me. Ralph and Sandy and Pat and I would spend most pay nights playing cards and drinking a goonie of "Red Ned" or Brown Muscat. We kept in touch for many years after Carboni St, but unfortunately, we no longer have contact.

Margaret must have been very confused during this period and couldn't come to grips with this stranger who would turn up for short periods and try to cuddle her and read her stories and take some of Mum's attention away from her. She would scream if I went near her and wouldn't stop till Mum or Aunty Sandy went to her. I tried everything and even took her into Liverpool with me to the shops. This only made matters worse because she would cling to anyone in greens and call them daddy, which caused some very strange looks from some soldier's wives. I finally couldn't handle this anymore, and after reading her a story one night through sobs and tantrums, I told her in stern terms that Mum was not going to come, and she'd better get used to it and went to storm out of the room. As I looked back, feeling like the lowest form of life, she sobbed, "I love you, Daddy," and I have to admit it made me cry like a kid, and I haven't done that often in my life. We were inseparable after that and she would wait for me to come home to play with her. She was my number one little girl until Robyn was born, and we had to go through it all again if she thought the baby was getting too much attention. I was slowly being taught by my children, and to this day they are still teaching me. The only difference now is that I have thirteen grandchildren to teach me as well.

Ralph and Sandy had the only car in the flats and would take us all shopping when we could afford it but having no car was becoming quite a nuisance, so I replied to an advert in the paper for a VW and asked our bank for a loan, which they refused because I had no credit record. I rang the chap back and told him the bad news. I'll never forget him for what occurred next. His name was Mick Hasham, and he picked Pat and I up and took us to see his bank manager at the CBC Bank in Chester Hill. No problems, we were told, but we will expect you to change your account to this bank. We didn't have to do a thing, the bank got us to sign the paperwork and gave us a cheque book to write out a cheque for Mick, and we drove off in our old but reliable VW.

I was still trying to get some answers regarding my engagement and the Married Quarter and notified the Orderly Room of our new bank details. Time marched on and we received a letter from the bank to say that they didn't mind honouring our cheques but would we please put some money in the bank. We had now reached critical stage and I began to demand answers, not excuses. A new lieutenant by the name of Pat Claque took over the investigation for us and we soon found out that Central Army Records Office (CARO) had not processed my application for engagement because I was not an Australian and had no Birth Certificate to prove who I was. In essence, they were saying that I was not allowed to be in their Army. This made me feel a little bit confused. Whose army had I been in for the past twenty-eight months if not "theirs"? The good Lt Claque was as perplexed as I was and there were some exchanges of fairly colourful language because CARO had informed the pay people that I had been discharged and they had stopped my bank allocation and we only had the money that I was getting through the Battalion. I suggested that we cancel the allocation and was told that we couldn't do that because my wife mightn't get any money if it wasn't allocated. Just how can you win with that sort of logic! I couldn't explain to them that she wasn't getting any money, so what rubbish were they talking? Someone in the pay system finally believed that I did exist and was still serving and released all of my back pay, which at least got the bank happy. Lt Claque somehow managed to have a Married Quarter allocated to us and we moved into 13 Derna Rd, Holsworthy Village, and almost at the same time, Ralph and Sandy bought a house in Campbelltown and moved into it.

Finally, in November 1970, the Army accepted a Statutory Declaration from my mother to say that I had really been born and allowed me into their army for a period of three years. We were living in a Married Quarter, had a car, were getting the correct level of pay and had been accepted into the army for three years. The system had worked, and we are forever indebted to Lt Pat Claque for all of his efforts.

Something must have been right in our lives because Pat was pregnant again. I was doing a Course at Studleigh Park near Narellan with my good mate Bobby Lyons. Another of those promotion courses and fairly intense. It was a closed camp which meant that we were not allowed to be away from the training centre during the period of training. Bob and I decided that we would slip away for a night and see the wives and children, and so we went to his house in the army village where Pat and Sue had a lovely meal cooked, and afterwards we adjourned to bed. Pat and Sue both fell pregnant that night, and our babies were born within hours of each other the following May.

Life was a series of Adventure Training, guard duties both in the Battalion and at HQ 2MD in Paddington, Signal Exercises, and other general Infantry training such as tactics and shooting. I was promoted to substantive Corporal and told that the chances of promotion to Sergeant were nil due to the number of discharges after Vietnam, bringing the number of positions available to almost none. Our life, whilst appearing to be good to those outside, was in fact starting to fall apart because of my stupidity, but I had not realised it yet.

I have been charged twice in my army career and both occasions were between 1970 and 1973, along with my only brush with the boys in blue. I didn't see any reason for the constant requirement to be a spit-polished soldier, and after being Guard Corporal for the umpteenth time and marching out to the rifle range to learn how to shoot and qualifying for a physical training test every three months, and the practice in between, and getting up at six o'clock to listen to some boorish PTI yelling at me in the gymnasium, and parades for this and that, and coffin bearer at military funerals. Surely the Army could find something less soul-destroying than this. Only two training stints had any variation, and they were the Adventure Training and signal exercises.

"Fun Run", it even sounds like something devised by an evil mind. We had many interesting little jaunts but the granddaddy of them all was a run from Sydney to Broken Hill. The idea was that there would be several teams of seven people in each team, and the first member of the team would run a mile then get in the bus until the other six ran a mile in turn, and then the first one would get out and run a mile, and so on until the team had covered forty-nine miles each day. From Sydney over the mountains and through to Nyngan, Cobar, Wilcannia, and Broken Hill. Get the key to the town and get pissed, then back on the buses and back to Holsworthy. There was undoubtedly some deep and meaningful reason to do that but I never quite understood it. Perhaps to instil teamwork or bonding or to keep fit or just because someone of importance thought it would be a really good idea. I can just imagine some junior officers in their Mess with a couple of red wines under the belt. "Letsh get the diggers to run to Broken Hill, tha should piss 'em orf, eh."

Signals Exercises kept me sane and I organised as many as I could. The idea was that groups of five or six would, under the supervision of a corporal, head off in all different directions and maintain communications with each other either directly or through relays, and after being on the road for four days we would meet at Sussex Inlet and discuss the problems that were encountered. Some would head north of Sydney and back, another would go west, another down the south coast, and I always went from Sydney to Braidwood and back to the coast via Nerriga and through Sassafras. Not very exciting you might say, but if you put yourself in my shoes, it was brilliant. Pat's parents were living on a little property near Nerriga and Pat would take the kids there whilst me and my crew went straight from Holsworthy to their house and put up a huge antenna and stayed there for four days. The diggers would go spotlighting and fishing and made themselves cosy little hutchies in a hayshed while I was inside with Pat and our girls. After four days, I would kiss Pat and the girls goodbye, and drive down through Sassafras to Nowra and then Sussex Inlet, where we would debrief and go to the RSL for light refreshments. Then it was back to Sydney to "make and mend" and spend the weekend at home with Pat and the girls. I suppose the Platoon Commander thought it strange the number of these that we wanted to do but probably thought that we were learning some valuable signal techniques and so condoned the fringe benefits. Besides, it gave him a week to himself without all those noisy little soldiers to annoy him. I also ran internal Signal Courses for the Company Sigs and as a result of all of this I became as good at my job as anyone in the battalion. It was just as well, for I was letting myself down badly in the discipline stakes.

I just couldn't get excited with all of the marching and duties required of me. Even when I wasn't in trouble, I managed to get into trouble. Let me explain. When a soldier is charged with some misdemeanour, he (there were no women in our unit) would be marched in front of the CO (Commanding Officer) to have justice meted out. To do this, there would be an Escort Party for the guilty soldier comprising of a front and rear escort and the RSM (Regimental Sergeant Major). One young lance corporal in my platoon had been AWOL (absent without leave) and was to front up. Who should be called upon as front escort but Corporal Bob Reed. The RSM gives all of the orders like quick march and left wheel and stuff and everything was going really well. I led the party down the path and into the passageway in the Headquarters Building and I should have known where the CO's office was but this was my first time as an escort and the doors to his office and the RSM's office were only inches apart, and the RSM gave the order to left wheel slightly late, and I led the party into his office and not the CO's. LCpl Springett was fined and stripped back to Private, which didn't concern him at all because he had already planned to go AWOL again straight away but wouldn't get caught this time, and I got three extra Guard Commanders, which I thought was unjust.

Guard duties were the most boring time possible. You spent all night playing cards and closing the OR's Canteen and making sure that the picquets were doing their rounds properly. The only thing worse than a guard was a guard with a Formal Guard Mount.

A formal mount meant that the battalion would be assembled to watch, and the whole thing was done with the band and all the big wigs watching. To be honest, I had done so many of them that it was becoming too easy for me. As well as the pomp and ceremony, there was an extra soldier in the guard, and when the Duty Officer inspected the guard he would nominate the best dressed soldier, who was allowed to have the night off, so all the lads would try really hard to be the best dressed. In truth, there was very little that could go wrong but if it did then I was always the bunny, or so it seemed. Again, let me give you an example. For those who are not familiar with army words of command, I apologise, but to explain each one would take a two-month course, and they are not that important. Suffice to say that we march on and stop in front of the dais, and the Duty Officer invites the CO (or his nominated person) to "Inspect the Guard."

All of this happened according to plan and a soldier was nominated as best dressed, mainly due to the amazing shine on his boots. The Guard and the band then march past the dais and the Guard Commander gives the order "Eyes Right" and the guard turns their heads to the right and the Commander salutes the officer taking the parade. Once more, all went to plan except that I was so used to this ceremony that instead of saluting on the stock of my rifle, I saluted with my left hand to my slouch hat. Being an old hand at these things, I did what good Corporals should and continued through the salute, gave the eyes front and marched the guard off the parade ground. Would you believe that only one person picked up my mistake? Not the RSM or the Adjutant or any of the big wigs. It was my Company Sergeant Major. I thought that I had got away with it until the next duty roster where I was surprised to see that Corporal Reed had two extra formal guard mounts. The CSM simply said, "Practise your saluting Reedy." Nothing else was ever mentioned. This was not the end of the bad luck because the soldier who had been given "Best Dressed" was the biggest grub in our platoon and had in fact forgotten to polish his boots and instead sprayed them with high gloss paint, and by the time we got to the guard house they had run everywhere and looked woeful. I pleaded with the Duty Officer to check them but he didn't, and the other diggers were so pissed off they gave me a hard time all night. The DO came up to the guard house later on and it was then that we noticed that he wore glasses but didn't have them on for the mount. All he could see was the shine, not the fact that they were still wet.

Margaret and Robyn were starting to develop their own little personalities and I thought that I was being a really good dad. Pat and I decided that we would have a boy and started to try again. To our dismay, nothing was happening and the more we tried, the less it worked. After finally visiting our local GP, a fine young doctor by the name of Dr Eddlestone, we were advised that everything was normal but perhaps we were trying too hard. He suggested that we abstain for a while and then try again. This was normal practice for an Infantry soldier anyway as we were often away from home for long periods, but we did try to relax a little, and I even stopped drinking for a few weeks. Still nothing occurred until out of the blue Pat informed me that she was pregnant again. Our little boy was on his way. As it turned out, Samuel turned out to be Samantha, and we had three beautiful little girls, and it didn't matter to me, although Pat's mum Beryl was extremely disappointed.

And this is how things were in that post-Vietnam period with me as the professional soldier and Pat as the dutiful wife and mother, and I believed that all was well with the world and we were a normal army household. Not enough money but managing with the Walton's repayments and Grolier Encyclopaedia repayments and having stews and casseroles on the off pays or when I lost the money at Rosehill or Harold Park or put too much through the pokies or over the bar at the soldiers' club or Wenty RSL. 1970 turned into '71, '72 and then 1973, and Pat could take the three girls shopping on the bus with Sam in the stroller with Rob tied to the stroller and Marg in a harness to prevent anyone doing a runner. She had groceries home delivered and the girls were always dressed nicely, and we always ate and had somewhere to sit and sleep. I helped out at home when I was there, which wasn't that often and Pat did the lot when she had to. With hindsight, it was going downhill and getting faster.

CHAPTER TWENTY-ONE

FROM IDIOT TO CIVI

There had been a series of largely unplanned and diverse lifestyles in my existence to contend with so far, the results of which had seen me halfway around the world, and as with most people, I could not have predicted any of it. I didn't recognise it at the time but a posting to Canberra was to change my life and it turned out to be so individually significant that it altered the direction in which the rest of my life was to progress. Up until now, there had not appeared to be any event, or events, that had caused me to consider anybody else in the way in which my lifestyle should progress. I hadn't looked for anything, and although there was much diversification, the contents of my life remained a series of adventures that unfolded around me as the principal, indeed only, player. Marriage and the arrival of our gorgeous girls had sown the seed for a change in attitude, but the lifestyle of an Infantry Corporal had resisted that change and had gone as far as to threaten what was a far more endearing lifestyle. I had not seen the need for me to change, and therefore it did not exist. Even up to the writing of this book, I had never realised or even considered that things had changed so drastically that it would cause me to take the bold action of splitting my life story into two parts.

Up until that time in late 1973, I had been like the parcel in a game of "pass the parcel". Round and round I would go, and then something would happen and the music would stop, another coat of veneer would be stripped from me, and I would emerge not as a beautiful butterfly but rather as another caterpillar. And each time that the music stopped, the caterpillar was getting uglier and more voracious with its family, and the cycle was getting quicker and quicker. I had become nomadic and obnoxious without realising it and had reached a point that left me restless after a short period in any one place, and we had been in Sydney for three years. Even marriage had not settled this desire to be constantly on the move. I identified it as a need for my "outside person" to satisfy their requirement, and it was slowly becoming a problem that I wouldn't allude to. To me, everything was fine and I was serving all masters at the same time and quite comfortably.

Pat had recognised that there was a problem and had started to make some demands on our relationship, which I had thought unreasonable at the time but with hindsight she was pretty close to the mark. Small things like not being as attentive to the girls' needs, staying in the Soldiers Club at Holsworthy far longer than I should, and getting irritated by insignificant things. We weren't on the verge of a total disaster, but there were signs there that I hadn't understood or recognised.

Vietnam had been and gone, and many of those people from that era had moved on also, whereas I remained at 5RAR and still went on exercises and training stints, and I had also developed the habit of drinking and gambling more heavily than we could afford, let alone the fact that I was being just plain stupid. I wanted to be on the go all the time and there was always going to be a point when it was going to bite me pretty hard if I continued in this vein.

To appease the gods, I had made many applications for a

transfer out of the Battalion and had been told, "It wasn't going to happen," but I kept them going in and hoped that something would turn up. I had always believed that any Infantry posting would be good enough for me and I hadn't considered my family even at this point. Possibly as some form of punishment, I found that I was always a popular choice to do the worst duties such as radio exercises and guard duties and organising platoon training, which again isolated me from Pat and the girls. To compound our problems, our gorgeous number three girl was imminent, and we were sure that she, would be a he. Sam turned out to be Samantha, but Pat and I didn't stress over that because she was healthy and so cute. Pat's mother Beryl was the most disappointed but she soon got over it and accepted another granddaughter. The fact that it had taken some time for Pat to fall pregnant should have added weight to my dilemma after being told that it was not the result of any physical problems but rather stress. I was a soldier; we didn't get stress, we were tough.

And then in late 1973 I received a Posting Order to Canberra as an Orderly to the Chief of Operations. My CO was so happy to get rid of me and even my RSM gloated that it was what I deserved for wanting to get out of "The Regiment." I had no idea what it meant to be an Orderly but Pat's face lit up like a Christmas Tree as it meant that she would be out of that army wives circle and out of the married quarters that we had fought so hard to get. I had missed the "small" things happening around me and hadn't even realised that Pat was not totally happy with the married quarter lifestyle but would tolerate most things to maintain the happy household. Such things as the time she joined a sewing class in the barracks and while chatting, as women do, she was informed that there was a "lady of ill repute," operating in the village at 13 Derna Road. In retrospect it is quite amusing, but the look of astonishment must have been so embarrassing when Pat informed her "confidante" that we lived at number 13 and that prostitution was not high on Pat's career path choices.

But I now know that this posting to Canberra was the turning point in my life and that it was to save my marriage and allow me to go on and function in the role of husband and father, or at least gave me a better opportunity to do so.

With three of the most beautiful girls in the world and my now not so agro wife, I was relocated to a house in the suburb of Lyneham in Canberra. There was only one other Army family there and in those days, Lyneham was a quiet, leafy suburb full of older families and ones like us with young parents and small children. Mum and Dad lived a mere half an hour away in Bungendore and I had a job with no stress and no weekend work and no guard duties or exercises or any other reason to be away from home. I was to all intents and purposes a civilian in uniform.

CHAPTER TWENTY-TWO

SEVEN TO FOUR

But before I run off at the mouth about all of this domestic bliss, I should first bring you up to date about this new posting that I "so richly deserved for being a traitor to the Regiment." In the power corridors of Russell Offices there are all of the people who make the decisions that result in the rest of us doing what we do. To help them in making these monumental decisions, the generals and civilian powerbrokers have their own personal staff who look after them while they get on with running the show. The Chief of Operations, one Major General A. L. MacDonald, had a Staff Officer, Major Rod Earl, a Personal Assistant Mrs Sandy Pettit and an Orderly, me. My role was to run messages all over the Russell Office Complex, make cups of tea, keep the General's office spick and span and generally help out as required. My direct chain of command was to Major Earl who was a happy-go-lucky Cavalry officer marking time in a necessary posting until a better one turned up. He had a natural revulsion of all things clerical and had soon passed on the task of upgrading the General's files to me, and if I do say so, I did it extremely well, and the recall satisfied the General and therefore the Major and therefore I wasn't a bad sort of a bloke. It was the start of a very rewarding clerical move in my next fifteen years of military service. This posting was not simply a change in my Army career path but was indeed a total change in lifestyle for our little family group. So, while my chances of promotion were no better now than in the Battalion, I had the bonus of being like a soldier in civvy street. I didn't know anyone who had been an orderly and so my role model was an old corporal whose main claims to fame included service in Korea, being the tea boy for the Chief of the General Staff and almost scalping himself on the feature wall in my lounge room. Corporal Lyle Evans was probably two hundred years old when I first met him and then got no older. To be honest, I never realised that making the occasional cuppa would be quite as involved as Lyle could make it. Of course we were dealing with generals here and so there were a number of protocols that needed to be observed. For example, I'll bet that you didn't think that I would breach some longstanding service ethic simply by a slight misjudgement of placement, but there you see, you would be wrong. Lyle instructed me in the use of the silver service before even my first sortie into the inner sanctum, to the point where I felt that I would have had no troubles serving *HRH* herself. His instructions left me with some major problems however, including overconfidence and a complete inability to use some initiative if the need arose. The second of these became apparent the very first time that I was called into action.

My general had been away for the first few days of my new posting and so I had had the opportunity to recce the office and plan my points of attack and this, coupled with Lyle's in-depth instructions, had me brimming with the self-confidence that only thorough planning can instil in individuals. For those of you who have never been in this most chilling of situations, imagine that you have been designated to clean the polar bear exhibit at Taronga Park Zoo and this was your first time and the bears are all at home. Not that I would ever insinuate that General A.L.

MacDonald resembled a polar bear, but I had heard that he ate brigadiers for breakfast. The moment that I lifted the silver tray, I knew that I was in all sorts of bother. What if I spilled it all over his desk, all over him, or if I was really lucky, what if I just fainted as I went through the door? I thought of running away or feigning some exotic disease. No, this was to be the real thing.

I pressed on for the few paces necessary to reach his office door, and while I was standing with this tray rattling like the Mallard through Thirsk station, to my absolute relief, Sandy opened the door with just the hint of a tap first. There he was, sitting at his desk, looking at me over his spectacles, no doubt appraising my worth or considering ways to have what was left of me posted to the worst possible place, and the first problem kicked in. He was not a tall man, but he exuded an aura that chilled those around him. He could tame wild lions with his gaze and was the epitome of what my maths master at school termed quietly frightening. I should have left instructions for the general to leave that area of his desk free that I would use to place the tray with the least possible number of obstructions. Damn it Lyle, you had failed me before I got started. But the nominated spot wasn't cleared of paperwork, and I was about to use some initiative, which was not covered in Lyle's instruction manual. Looking around, I decided on the coffee table and proceeded with the assistance of the shaken cups and saucers to place the tray there, from whence I would pour the tea, serve and graciously bow and scrape in retreat. He again looked over his spectacles, and I got the impression he had decided to boil me in oil rather than waste bullets. And so, I righted the cups and saucers and poured with just a dash of milk, and I placed his cuppa on a coaster beside his blotting pad and stood back waiting for the accolades that would surely follow. The second problem then kicked in, and with the overconfidence of an infantry buffoon, I spoke. A simple question asking, "Would that be all, sir?" So very like "Upstairs, Downstairs." He had mumbled something that I hadn't understood and not wishing to appear ignorant, I continued my retreat, and realising that this was to be a daily ritual for the duration of my tenure hoped that with a little bit of luck he would decide on the guillotine and not the boiling oil.

It was some ten minutes later that the major caught up with me and gave me a bit of a serve. Those mumbled few words from my general were not, surprisingly, meant as undying gratitude for an excellent cuppa but rather his request that I send the Major in to his office. Of course I apologised profusely and vowed that there would be no repeat and thanked my lucky stars that Major Rod Earl was a really good bloke.

The posting to Army Office lasted until 1978 and it indeed changed me from what could have been a lifetime of undying support for the Royal Australian Regiment and all that that entailed to a clerical-based career path and more importantly, although I couldn't recognise it then, it was the start of my life as a man with a family and the emphasis changed for me as of then. Nothing was done because I wanted it, but rather I started to think of the ramifications for the kids and Pat and Mum and Dad, and Pre School parents and all of those wonderful and diverse people who were to contribute to my life. And for all of you who must know, yes, I did spill a cuppa one day and it was on Major General A. L. MacDonald's desk when he was the Vice Chief of the General Staff and he didn't boil me in oil but rather he said, "Better get a cloth and clean that up Corporal Reed." So you see we were then on a first name basis.

My military career had taken off at a huge tangent, which no longer required me to think like a soldier. Mundane everyday stuff like what to have for lunch and delivering that document to so and so and ensuring that the General's drink flask was full and filing some documents were the fulcrum points around which I balanced each day. My skill in the clerical field was hardly setting the world on fire but I was being asked to spend more time in the Coord Offices where the real administration was done and I was learning something each day.

My military commitment was so constantly seven to four that I was able to moonlight for a period of time by doing cleaning at Fyshwick with Monier Roof Tiles. Each afternoon I would head off to Monier at four o'clock and clean their factory for five hours, then home and dinner. The work was hard but enabled us to "get ahead" and satisfied the need to keep physically active instead of sitting in an office all day.

For those of you who have not experienced the day-to-day life of a soldier and his family in an Infantry Battalion, I will try to paint a picture of how I saw it. For the nights that I was home, there was always something of a military nature to do such as ironing parade clothing, spit-polishing boots, preparing lesson plans for a course that I was conducting, checking and packing "bush" gear for an exercise, having a beer at the canteen, or going to the club with my mates. There were many periods that I wasn't home for two, three, four weeks or more. In fact, Pat and I once sat down and calculated my absences, and in my first five years of military service, I was away from home for three of them. Pat had lived in a caravan park in Milperra, boarded with friends on a chook farm, rented a house in Queanbeyan with her brothers and an uncle, moved back to Sydney into a flat in Liverpool, a married quarter at Holsworthy Village, and now to a rented house in Canberra. She had given birth to three children and looked after their needs with only the public transport system to travel on. Even on the nights when I was "home" I was moonlighting by shovelling chook shit at Appin to try and make ends meet and support my drinking and gambling.

The physical demands on an infantry soldier were quite unique by way of the endurance and stamina requirements and not simply strength. Anyone who has experienced the Jungle Training Centre in Queensland will know the true meaning of "heartbreak hill" when just as you think you have reached the top another crest appears. I have seen big strong men break down and weep with frustration, as the top never seems to materialise. The endless parades and mundane periods of "hurry up and wait" and "greatcoats on, greatcoats off" and "everyone on the truck, everyone off the truck." Infantry battalions in peace time were great planners but woeful organisers. They probably invented such things as "time safety factors" and "just in case" as opposed to "just in time." I hope that today's infantry soldiers don't have the same trials and tribulations and that their training is more diverse and rewarding than it used to be.

And that was how my first five years of military service developed. Now I had a "job" and started at seven and finished at four. There were no parades or exercises, no more rifle ranges or close training areas, no guard duty or mess duty. I wore a uniform each day but it was either service dress or poly's. When I got home at night, I had no military stuff to do and instead I could play with the kids and talk to my wife. I had already sworn off gambling, and now I would enjoy a beer at home. We visited Pat's family almost every weekend and did our shopping together. This was bliss for Pat, and I was getting used to it pretty quickly. If I seem to be labouring on my family's new direction then I apologise, but it really was such a dramatic change of lifestyle.

The posting to Army Office in Canberra went from September '73 to September '78, and in that time I advanced from Infantry Corporal to Ordnance Staff Sergeant, and got a cushy posting to Townsville at the end of it.

CHAPTER TWENTY-THREE

DOMESTIC BLISS

During the agricultural days at Lanyon Station, I was always fascinated by the prominence of the veggie garden in the everyday lives of all the people there, whether it was the monster garden at the homestead or the patches around each of the cottages. They ranged from ones that rivalled the best market gardens to supply the whole property to a couple of tomato plants surrounded by radishes gone to seed. They were something that I had seen in England, and as back then, they were the topic of many conversations. Indeed, they ranked right up there with football, sex, politics, and work. How well your tomatoes or pumpkins performed in the global scheme of things could determine your status for years to come. The new varieties, shapes and sizes of vegetables were endless. In particular, men boasted of the size of their produce, and I have since wondered if there is some substitute part of the male anatomy that was at stake in this boasting. Anyway, the veggie garden was and still is an important part of the male ego.

I would have to be honest and declare that my attempts at producing sufficient food for our existence had, up until the summer of '73–74, been modest at best. I had made efforts to scratch at the barren married quarter soils before but had never achieved any real success. Unless you counted ten thousand split and tough radishes I had, in fact, been a dismal failure. What I needed was some influence in my gardening efforts, a partner in crime, someone with a green thumb and a strong back. Enter Mr Robert Perrott. Robert had developed from an adventurous outdoors teenager into an adventurous outdoors young man with a penchant for a cold drink on a hot day. He was the original loveable larrikin, and he had a green thumb, and he had come to live with us on and off. Although the Flea, as he was nicknamed, has now unfortunately passed away, I am sure he would agree that he lived with us when he was in trouble for something and not with us while he was getting into trouble for something. He was always something of a free spirit and enjoyed the three Fs— fishing, fighting, and you know the other one. But at that time, most importantly, he had a green thumb, in fact, he could almost be a Martian.

We shared the hard work of digging the garden beds and preparing them for planting, but the process became out of control because while one was digging and the other preparing, neither of us made the decision to stop, and as a consequence, an area of some ninety square meters of veggie garden appeared with a fence to keep out the undesirables such as Fred the dog and the kids and the ferrets. It stretched the full width of the back yard and some three meters in from the back fence. It was right up there with the pyramids and the Suez Canal as a feat of engineering brilliance.

If there is a vegetable known to man, we probably had three rows of them. Apart from onions, everything flourished. I make particular note of the onions for a special reason that will become apparent much later. We had broken into the "market garden" level of garden and I was soon taking bags full of produce into work. It got so bad that people would put off doing their shopping until after the Monday morning delivery. They were starting to rely on the veggie run.

Everyone in our household wanted to jump on the bandwagon. Pat would stand proudly watering the marvel in our backyard whilst soaking up the acclaim of the neighbours who declared, "I haven't seen anything quite like it."

"Would you like some tomatoes?" she would silkily taunt. "We have plenty, and it would be a shame to waste them."

Off the neighbours would toddle and fetch a bag, saying, "Don't put in too many or we won't be able to eat them all," and "How about a few of those lovely beans too?" The kids would climb in and pull carrots and pick peas and tomatoes then wash them under the tap and eat them raw. They were nearly as good as lollies—nearly. Often would be heard the lady of the house admonishing the girls with, "You kids get out of the garden."

Flea and I would now relinquish all ownership of the garden until the next year when the preparations over with, we would plant the next generation of vegetables with the appropriate composting and attention to the worm farm, which brings me to the next newish activity—fishing.

Having always been a keen but non-practising fisherman except for the period at Lanyon, I was very keen to renew the hobby. The Murrumbidgee was only a short drive away either at Lanyon or towards Burrinjuck Dam, and although European Carp had already made some inroads into our waterways, there were still enough trout to keep us occupied. The other huge advantage now was that Pat and the girls all loved to get out into the fresh air and so we could "family fish." Marg, Rob, and Sam spent most of their time reeling in and trying to cast their lines out. Attending to their needs was no longer a chore, but rather heaps of fun, and they stayed at home on occasion to allow Dad and Uncle Bob to do some serious fishing. Fishing had another special advantage in that it allowed our family group to go camping and fishing as well. All of my children loved to go camping, and they were in no way squeamish about creepy crawlies or getting dirty.

Although we had many camping expeditions during the Lyneham period, there was one particular trip that really highlights the fun we were having as a family. It was an Easter break and we went along the Murrumbidgee River close to the village of Tharwa and Cuppacumalong Hereford Stud property. It was like tent city, and even John Hamilton ventured out during the days. There was a huge "kitchen tent" in the middle of the camp and all the sleeping tents were strewn around it and the campfire, which was regularly stoked up. Flea and I caught rabbits, and we all caught fish and ate like kings. Marg and Rob did almost everything that I did and never complained about being tired or dirty—in fact, we couldn't keep either of them clean, and so just accepted that they were as they were. Sam was too young to be as involved unless she was carried, and Tim was only a small baby at the time, but the weather was perfect, and the fresh air did them no harm at all.

On the Easter Sunday, I learned another tradition and again saw the wonderment and happiness on the faces of my children. It was, of course, the Easter egg hunt. We adults hid what seemed like millions of small chocolate eggs all around and just outside of the camp area and then let the children go wild. Lorraine was there and my brother David with his little ones, and the adults followed behind to make sure that all of the eggs were found. "Don't eat them all now!" was heard often but it didn't make much difference to hungry children who left a trail of tinfoil wrappers wherever they went. I have always tried to instil a sense of fairness in the kids but I have to admit Margaret and Robyn had a distinct advantage because I think they may have had a sneaky peak when the eggs were being hidden, but I didn't try to stop their triumphs and they did share with Sam without too much hinting. After the hunt was over and all the others had gone home with their chocolate-covered kids, we settled back and sat next to the fire and replayed the day over and over, with Flea and I enjoying a relaxing Port. Marg and Rob listened to each tall story that was told and poked the fire with sticks, and even though they were admonished by Mum, Dad was a softy and said, "They'll be all right," through a warm Port glow. They made the sparks fly like a fireworks' display, and laughed at Fred the dog as he tried to catch each of the flying embers. This was the life. Mention of Fred the dog reminds of the pets that we had in the Lyneham dynasty.

We had a dog in the Holsworthy village but the children were too young to appreciate him and he was quite a cranky little Terrier. Unfortunately, he was given a bait and passed on and we didn't get another until we were in Lyneham.

Les and Beryl had some friends in Queanbeyan who had pups that they were trying to give to a good home and so I was conned to taking everyone to check them out. "We are not getting one," said I, "We are only going to look at them and see what they are like." Can you imagine how stupid that sounds in retrospect? The puppies were Bassett crossed with about thirty other breeds but they were the cutest little things and the Bassett really stood out with the most adorable little faces. Of course their father had said no and so the kids didn't make a fuss or protest too much—as if. They pleaded and said please a thousand times and promised to look after it and love it and cuddle it and that it wouldn't be any trouble or make messes that had to be cleaned up. I, of course, being the master of the household, stood firm with my decision not to have a puppy but knew that I had lost this argument, and so it was that we left with this little ball of fun and the girls were as happy as Larry. We agonised over a name, but I eventually won that battle and naturally, with the Bassett being predominant, he was called Fred.

Within a couple of days, Fred became quite ill to the point that I feared he would not survive and already there was much crying and gnashing of teeth. "Is there nothing we can do?" pleaded Pat and the girls. I remembered that there was a vet who had done a lot of work for Lanyon, and his surgery was close, so we took little Fred to Norm Boluss and let him examine him. The news was not good, and Fred was diagnosed as having distemper, and the vet suggested that we leave him there to have the long sleep. "Surely there is something that can be done," Pat cried to the vet, who saw the tears in two little girls' eyes and suggested that he give Fred some injections and that we take him home and keep him warm and totally inactive and quiet and feed him sweet cream biscuits and give him lots of clean water.

"If it works it will be a miracle," said the vet, but we tried anyway. It was almost impossible to keep the girls away from him and I was constantly telling them to leave him alone. In their defence they only wanted to cuddle him and nurse him back to health and they kept his water clean and fed him broken sweet cream biscuits and cleaned up his little jobs. To my surprise the little fellow seemed to be improving but I played the devil's advocate and didn't let anybody get their hopes up. The girls kept telling me that he was getting better and that he would be all right. It was almost as if it was scripted that he indeed did make a full recovery and was soon tumbling around the back yard on his stubby little legs and jumping all over the kids, but I can never ever remember him barking. Fred did make a full recovery and lived a long and happy life until he was given a glass bait many years later that was ironically given in a sweet cream biscuit.

A more faithful dog I have never had nor a luckier one. He loved the car and came everywhere with us but most of all he loved hunting rabbits. In all of his life he only ever caught one and it was blind with Mixo and he didn't know what to do when he ran it down. But as a ferreting assistant, he was brilliant. Not a tussock or log or bush would be left unexplored, and the rabbits would dash off into their burrow with Fred in hot pursuit. Along the hills around Lake George, we ferreted and would get up to twenty pairs a day, which we sold through a butcher where Flea worked for one dollar each, which paid for the fuel to get out to Bungendore and perhaps a nice cold drink. Hiscocks in Queanbeyan would buy all of the best skins, and the hide man took the rest but rooked us every time.

Fred was the best natured dog that we have had, including the scaredy-cat Belgian Shepherd named Missy that we currently have. He loved the kids and the ferrets, and we would all roll around the backyard playing. When I say all, I mean Pat and I with Robert, the three girls and later baby Tim, Fred and the two ferrets, Arthur, and Charcoal. And he did have more lives than a cat. Some of his escapes included jumping into burning tussocks, having a tree fall across his back, being stolen and finding his way home three months later with his pads worn off and bleeding, getting thrown out of a car that had rolled over and over, being lost in the Ansett freight system en route to Townsville, swimming in the ocean at Saltwater creek shortly after the sighting of a three metre shark, falling out of the tree that he used to climb to get out of the yard, and most painful of all having his testicles caught in a diamond chain fence trying to get to the bitch across the road.

There were so many new and wonderful things at Lyneham, and Christmas finally had some real meaning for me. The kids' eyes when they saw their presents from Santa at the bottom of their bed and the beer and cake left for the old man in red. The family sharing in the decorations and the laughter, and even the squabbles, were magic for me too. Pat and the girls would make some decorations from all sorts of material, and those decorations were better than all of the glitzy bought ones. Even today, I see the look in my grown-up children's eyes as they decorate their homes with their children, and so it will be with their children's children. Watching our girls playing with friends and seeing their eyelids struggling to stay open when it was story time at night and teaching them to ride pushbikes and watching them jump into the swimming pool off my bedroom window and so many other things. I even enjoyed sports weekends.

All of our girls played hockey, and I was still playing football (soccer), which led to the most hectic of weekends in the winter months. First things on Saturday morning it was bedlam in the Reed household with cleaning up, bed making, breakfast, and getting everyone's gear ready. Then it was into the car and off to the first hockey venue and drop Margaret and Pat off, then the next venue and drop Robyn off, and then somewhere else for me and Sam, and I stayed to watch her game. The pick-up was in the reverse, and all the way it was gibber, gibber, gibber with excited little voices or complaints of getting hit with the ball or sticks. Back home for a quick lunch, then off again to watch Dad play football and eventually home again. Dinner, bath, and watch TV until bedtime and story reading, kiss them all goodnight and listen for the giggles before total peace and then bedlam again on Sunday morning. There is something enjoyable about being woken at sparrow on a Sunday morning by giggling children jumping on you. At least there was then.

Sunday we usually went to Nan and Pop Perrott's house at Bungendore for the day. Pat's mum and dad are fairly old-fashioned and they loved to see little girls dressed in frilly stuff and not jeans and tee shirts but putting Margaret and Robyn in dresses at Bungendore was the same as wearing a tuxedo to a rodeo. They were very much the explorers and would get into all sorts of places to get dirty and have fun. It must have been terrible for nan and pop trying to make them be little girls, and no doubt it was not fun for the girls either. But we mostly enjoyed our times with Les and Beryl and the rest of the family and managed to fit a few projects in like renewing the lounge room floor and painting the kitchen and stuff like that. After all day at Bungendore, it was back in the car and home to dinner and bed once more.

Some weekends when the weather was just too bad to go out, we would kick back in front of the fire and listen to liquorice discs on the turntable. With fire burning and everyone comfortable to the sounds of Queen, Skyhooks, all of the Liverpool sounds, David Bowie, Slade, Pink Floyd, Sherbet and The Scrum Halves. "The Scrum Halves," you say, "Who are they?" Well, after some beer and hot chillies and salami, we may have inadvertently played some rugby songs, but that ceased after a call from Margaret's school. "Mrs Reed, your daughter has disgraced herself at show and tell today and we need to talk to you straight away." Poor Pat had to go and get the inquisition because of my stupidity. As with all children, they seem to learn the things that we don't want them to better than anything else, and it would appear that for show and tell, Margaret had simply burst into a song that her dad played on the weekend when we all sat around the fire and listened to music. "Arse holes (Our souls) are fresh today etc, etc", followed by her rendition of The Ram from Derbyshire. Her total innocence should have told those of authority that this was not a case of a child racing off into a world of decadence but then, it was not the first time we had been called to the school.

I have never believed in telling lies to my children or trying to "protect" them from things in life which, whilst not always commonplace, are facts of normal life in the rural environment. When Les worked on a property on the hills above Bungendore, part of his job description was the Artificial Insemination (AI) of the herd of Simmental cattle. As a consequence, the girls were allowed to watch this procedure and I tried, as best as I could in language that they could understand, to explain what Pop Perrott was doing. Of course Margaret was full of wide-eyed excitement at this and sure enough, come Monday morning it was, "Mrs Reed, can you come to the school straight away." Margaret's explanation of AI went something like, "My Pop put on this really long plastic glove and with a tube in his hand, stuck his arm right up a cow's bum up to here," as she indicated an area near her shoulder. "Dad said he was trying to get her pregnant so she could have a cute little calf." No matter how hard Pat and then I tried to explain what had happened, we were always viewed as a sort of perverted hillbilly family and at P&C Meetings people would give us wide berths, and there was always a vacant seat near us even if some people had to stand. I have to say that Pre School wasn't as bad, and I was even the secretary of that organisation for a short time. The only male with all these young mums and teachers. Who said Pre School was boring?

Our youngest offspring, Timothy Robert Reed, was born in May 1976, delivered by caesarean section and somewhat premature. It is probably testament to how content I was at that time that Tim was conceived totally unplanned and with only one missed pill, whereas Sam's conception took ages. Pat was quite ill and Tim was kept in a Humidicrib for nearly three months, and so the role of mother to the girls fell on Dad. During the days, the family across the road from us would look after them and I would pick them up after work. I would take them home and prepare and eat dinner and they would get in the bath while I did some basic cleaning. While I showered and got dressed, the girls would dress themselves. It was the one area that I allowed them complete autonomy and they would come up with some of the most amazing fashion statements ever. People in the hospital would have bets on what they would wear next, and Pat would say, "Please dress the girls properly to bring them in."

"But they are clean and happy," I would reply, and they looked gorgeous in long-legged multi-coloured socks, tights under party dresses and whatever else made them feel good. All of that fun stopped when Pat brought Tim home and our family group was complete.

Our son is now a large man who loves nothing better than putting his head into rugby scrums as a tighthead prop, but as a baby he was a weedy little thing and always looked to be half-starved. Pat and I would worry ourselves sick at his lack of weight gain and couldn't come to grips with the fact that he would always seem to be hungry no matter what we provided. All of the girls were good "doers" and we had no trouble with them at all. It was some time before we got to the bottom of the problem, and it was by sheer accident. All three of the girls seemed to adore Tim and always wanted to do things for him such as take him for walks in the stroller and play with him, and in particular they loved to give him his bottle and baby food, which

Pat either made up from vegetables or bought cans of goodies such as puree fruit and other yummy stuff. In fairness to Sam, she was probably an innocent but willing participant at feeding times. I thought that I would check to see how they were all progressing with the feeding, as I had on other occasions, but I must have approached with less noise this time. They were in one of the bedrooms when I arrived and then knew what the problem was. It was simply a case of "One for Tim, one for me, one for Robyn and one for Sam." Even with the bottle, Tim was only getting one quarter of the food that we provided. I couldn't seem to get mad at the girls and we soon rectified the problem, and although we didn't stop them from tasting the food, we made sure that Tim got enough to increase his growth rate.

I have never been big into parties except for the kids' birthdays and special days, and so we rarely had any great gatherings at our house but rather we went to other people's places for parties. This suited me, being basically antisocial, because there were no messes to clean up and I could leave whenever I was ready, which was a disappointment to Pat quite often, but that's the way I am. We did have one memorable BBQ at 96 Longstaff St Lyneham and it was what you might term "a really good do." We invited everyone that we knew, including the neighbours and Flea's mates, and they all turned up. The night was a beautiful late spring evening with the BBQ on for anyone who wanted to cook something and a fire bucket made from an old washing machine shell and tub. The beer flowed like water, and with the exception of one small incident everyone got on with no arguments. The incident occurred early in the evening when Flea noticed all of the young ones crowded around one end of the vegetable garden, and they were obviously excited about something. It was one of Flea's young mates and his girlfriend performing horizontal PT in the middle of the spinach patch. Of course we couldn't allow that to continue, so they were removed from the premises. Can you imagine the damage they could have done to the spinach?

After that episode, everyone got stuck in and the night was an absolute cracker. At some point during stage two I had a bet with one of Flea's mates that I could put a ferret down my trouser leg and let it come out at the bottom. He, of course, doubted this and declared that I should show him and a couple of his mates how it was done. Only being at stage two gave me enough courage to perform this act which could, if it went wrong, save me the need for a vasectomy. I did have two advantages however and they were that I knew and had handled the ferret for a long time and I had tracksuit pants on. Boldly to the cage I strode and extracted Charcoal who was one of two that played in the yard with the kids and the dog. Back into the firelight so that they could see that nothing was up my sleeve, so to speak, and with much bravado pulled the trackie pants open as far as possible and placed Charcoal in at a point well past the family jewels. The ferret did what he was trained to do and followed the tunnel made by the pants, and I opened the elastic at my ankles and out he came thinking that that was the shortest burrow he had been in. I picked him up and gave him a scratch then returned him to his cosy cage. Unbeknown to me, this young lad was well past stage three and he had made a substantial bet with one of my army friends that he could put a ferret down his trouser leg. Steve, my army friend, took the wager and the young lad strolled over to the cages to get the ferret. His problem was that he had not taken enough notice of which one I had used, and as a consequence, he tried to pick up the female named Martha. Now Martha's role in the organisation was to produce young ferrets and she was never handled and had the temperament of a wolverine with a toothache. The night air was suddenly filled with the most terrifying scream that I have ever heard and upon looking up, I saw this chap running around the yard with Martha firmly attached to two fingers, and anyone who knows ferrets will know that they do not let go easily. Luckily, Flea was able to tackle him to the floor and grabbed Martha behind the head and by blowing up her nose made her release the fingers. After Pat had administered first aid and severely admonished me and her brother, she arranged for someone to take the lad home. His problems had not finished however because Steve caught up with him and demanded that he pay up for not achieving the bet. The poor lad never came back to our house.

My mentor in the art of tea service was at this grand function and he had consumed a large amount of all sorts of alcohol. So much so that it was decided to get him a taxi back to Duntroon before he passed out. I took him inside to the fire in the lounge room and gave him what he thought was another drink but was in fact water with a sniff of gin. The lounge room at Lyneham was almost as long as a cricket pitch and we were at the fireplace situated at the farthest point from the front door. So that when the taxi arrived, Lyel had to negotiate that distance to reach the door. He started off well enough, being upright and placing one foot in front of the other in the correct sequence. As he progressed, he leaned increasingly forward, and the sequence of his feet began to become erratic at best. By the time he reached the area near the front door he had become almost horizontal and was travelling at something approaching the speed of sound. Again, luck was with me but not Lyel because the wall that he head-butted was a brick feature wall and the only damage was to his head. I asked the taxi to wait a couple of minutes while we revived poor Lyel and administered bandages, then escorted him to the taxi, paid the driver and gave him the Duntroon Barracks address. Lyel did survive but he told me on Monday that he must have been mugged on his way home because he woke up with a splitting headache and severe lacerations and bruising to his bonce.

By now the party had advanced to the point that some of the female partners were urging their males to retire for the evening and go home before dawn broke. Those of us who were left invented a new way to create carnage. We created a racetrack from somewhere in the backyard, down the side of the house around a rockery and back into the backyard finishing point. At first there were some solo timed runs performed on the kids' three-wheel trikes but soon these became competitive races of three in each race. After more band aids and Dettol, I reached stage five and went to bed. I don't know what time it all finished but I remember waking up to find a strange man in bed with Pat, and I and not being able to get into the toilet because Beryl, Pat's mum, was asleep in there behind the door. It took all of Sunday to put the house and yard back into shape and get all of the bodies fed and sent home, and so many people wanted to know when we were having our next BBQ.

Our time at Lyneham was indeed a turning point and especially so for me. I was happy and content and had learned so much about being a father and husband. This was nothing that most people hadn't already known, but I had never experienced the simple joys of children's laughter, the almost endless questions and problems that required the wisdom of Solomon to untangle. When your children snuggle up to you in the mornings or jump on you to play, the look of amazement as you read them stories and try to bring the characters to life and then the peaceful time when you can watch them sleeping. I could, and still do, enjoy a cold drink on a hot day, but the gambling was finished apart from the occasional ten dollars in the pokies with Pat. I was still a soldier with all that that entailed but it was no longer the main focus for me. From then onwards I tried to be a better father/husband and although I have no doubt made many mistakes since then, they were all made trying to do the best that I could.

CHAPTER TWENTY-FOUR

MILITARY PROGRESSION

I no longer had that Infantry mindset and was becoming more involved with matters clerical instead, but still wore the red lanyard on the Infantry shoulder and the Infantry shoulder bars. As I became more proficient with making cups of tea and running errands, there was time to sit in the Coordination Office and observe and learn. Truth is that I had a natural bent for that type of work but had never realised it. It was not long before I was given some clerical tasks to do, and the more I did, the more I was given. I have to admit that I had a fine teacher in WO2 Mike Johnson who, although an annoying practical joker, taught me that in any clerical position, accuracy was the most important factor. I must have been reasonably good at what I was doing because the powers that be decided that there was sufficient work to create a position and I was "advised" that I should consider a Corps Transfer to Ordnance in the clerical stream. If that was to happen then it was highly probable that I would get to fill the new position.

My application for Corps Transfer and attendance at a Basic Clerical Course went in and I soon found myself in Randwick in Sydney doing the course. About now was the first time that I had some doubts about this clerical stuff. Part of the syllabus was to learn to type thirty words a minute without any mistakes on the old Olivetti typewriters. Homework consisted of typing A4 sheets, leaving no margins, of practice typing. Have you any idea how long it takes to fill pages of asdf asdf asdf and hjkl hjkl hjkl? Boring and mindless doesn't even begin to describe it. The rest of the course was easy and at the end I was a clerk in Ordnance Corps and was promoted to Temporary Sergeant pending completion of an Advanced Clerical Course. Becoming a sergeant meant more money of course but it also made me a member of the Army Office Sergeants' Mess and the junior member at that.

Army messes are something like a cross between an exclusive club and the early opener in Liverpool lovingly called "The Chevron Rails." Anyone who lived in the area then will appreciate the comparison. The epitome of this comparison is a function called "The Formal Dining-In Night." And the junior sergeant in the mess plays an important if not frightening part of the proceedings on these nights. My luck ran true to form and the next such night was planned before another corporal was promoted and I got the job of "Mister Vice."

A brief explanation of the structure of Army Sergeants' Messes for the uninitiated. All of the sergeants and warrant officers in a unit or military area are automatically members of the Mess, which is presided over by a senior Warrant Officer Class One. This group of soldiers are called Senior Non-Commissioned Officers (SNCOs) and the senior member is called the President of the Mess Committee (PMC). The social calendar for the Mess includes some Formal Dining-In Nights and some mixed nights with wives or partners. The junior member of the Mess has certain duties at these functions so that they can learn the protocols and generally be held to ridicule, as is the Army's British heritage.

I had never been into a mess as a member and so I asked a

million questions as to my role, and the more I asked the more rubbish I was told. The PMC gave me a "formal briefing" and from all of this I gleaned that I was to sit at the end of one of the table arms by myself and facing the official party. I was to ensure that everyone was in the dining room by a given time, say Grace and toast the Queen. At the end of the dinner, I was to sit in the PMC's chair and control the proceedings while the official party retired for cigars, coffee, and other delights. In a normal mess situation, there would be possibly fifty or so members but in Army Office there are hundreds, and I was wishing that I was still a Corporal.

The big night arrived and I donned my new mess kit, admired myself in the mirror looking like something out of an old British movie and headed off about an hour early as my training had instilled the time safety factor into my brain. I walked through my role for the night and as more people arrived, I got more and more nervous to the point that I was feeling physically ill. It would be wise to mention that in those early days of my mess life the PMC did not allow anyone to leave the dining room until after the meal was finished and the room cleared, and one of my duties was to let everyone know when we were ten minutes from entering the dining room so that they could empty their bladders and/or throw one last drink down before the meal. So far it was going really well and although I had completed only one small task it was done with aplomb and my confidence soared. It was like playing football when all the nerves went after the kick-off. Once again it was overconfidence that brought me undone. At the appointed time, I announced that everyone was to enter the dining room and stand at their allocated seating while I went to the toilet and made sure that it was empty and no one was hiding in there. Getting a couple of hundred SNCOs who had spent the last hour trying to drink the bar dry to their allocated seats was a logistics exercise equalled only by Hannibal getting all those elephants over the Alps. Finally, with everyone sorted out, I reported to the PMC that the mess was assembled so that he and the official party could be piped into the dining room by a lone bagpiper. Then it was rush back into the room to stand by my seat and bring the mess to attention for the official party.

But my chair had mysteriously disappeared and I started to think what was I going to do when everyone else sat down. Whilst thinking about this the official party was standing in the doorway with the Piper playing and waiting to be announced. "Oh shit!" I thought and finally called the mess to attention. The party moved to their places and the PMC boomed out "Mr Vice, Grace." I had forgotten about Grace and the words were not in my head. "Lord" that was a good start I thought, whilst also thinking, "Where's me fucking chair?" Some adlibbing got "Please bless those assembled, and," thinks, "I might have to just squat and pretend to be sitting but that's going to be pretty hard," then, "The food that we are about to eat Amen." There were muttered amens from around the room and the official party took their seats followed by all of the mess members. I am eternally grateful to the mess steward who appeared with a chair for me, and I sat, relaxed.

I think the meal was very good but in truth I don't remember it, but there was a huge amount of wine consumed while I remained as sober as a judge. I could never understand that saying, as I now believe that judges are no more sober than anyone else. There was one other task that I was required to perform before taking over from the PMC, and that was to propose the toast to the Queen. Once again, at the appointed time, I arose, with one foot hooked onto my chair and said,

"Gentlemen, please be upstanding for the Royal Toast." I had, by being gender-specific, offended some of the women present, which I was to pay for later. When all were upstanding, I proposed the toast with vigour by raising my glass to the portrait of HRH and in a loud voice saying, "The Queen." There was a general muttering throughout but to my immediate right there was a distinct Scottish voice which whispered, "Fuck the Queen, and that Greek bastard wi' her." I burst out with uncontrolled laughter and looked up to see the PMC staring at me with his eyebrows raised almost to his receding hairline with that "What do you think you're playing at" look, or perhaps it was that "I think I will remove your testicles with a dessert spoon" look.

The rest of the dinner went without problem until the PMC announced that the official party were going to retire and that Mr Vice should take the Chair. Up until now there had been vast amounts of wine consumed but no one was game enough to ask the PMC if they could go to the toilet. Bladders would have been at bursting point and I knew that there were going to be a lot of requests for a toilet break. Whispering into the PMC's *shell like* I asked if we could have a toilet break. "No way, keep them here for fifteen minutes and then let them go," he asserted and left the dining room.

One saving grace was that I was allowed to take two other people with me to the "King Table" and had arranged for two experienced Warrant Officers to escort me. But I had this awful feeling that after only being promoted for a couple of weeks that I was way out of my depth.

Someone stood up and called out, "Mr Vice, I think I speak for everyone here that we collectively need a piss!"

"Err, sorry about that, but youse will have to wait," I whispered.

The Warrant on my right whispered in my ear and I screamed out for Sergeant so and so to stand on the table and tell a joke. The Sergeant stood and declared that he didn't know any. "Then make one up or sing us a song," I replied. The room became rowdy and boisterous, and I called, "Gentlemen, some quiet for the song." One older female stood up and declared that I was a sexist pig and how dare I call her a gentleman. The warrant on my right spoke up, "Even if you were male, we couldn't call you a gentleman," followed by more laughter and bandying of words. Finally, the fifteen minutes were over and I declared that everyone could leave the dining room.

In all my life I have never witnessed what happened next. There was a stampede that had bodies jammed in doorways, the toilets couldn't accommodate the numbers that needed to go and the grassed areas were soon wet enough to bog a billycart. Even the women were squatting out there. How these people had managed to wait this long I will never know and it was just as well that there were no "after dinner games" as is usual or else there would be more saturation to follow. I checked with the PMC before going home, he gave me another of those looks and told me to report to his office first thing on Monday morning. When I got home, I told Pat all about it and she was amazed at the night's events. All weekend I sweated it, until Monday morning and I went to the PMC's office. The PMC was also the Regimental Sergeant Major (RSM) for all of Army Office and I was sure that my short reign as a sergeant was about to be terminated followed by a posting to anywhere that was really bad.

"Ah, Sergeant Reed," he said. "A good night on Friday and I think you handled it very well. Jock usually throws people with his tirade against the Queen, and missing chairs has caused more problems than you had."

"I thought I was in it up to here," I said, indicating an area about a foot above my head.

"A good learning curve son," and he actually smiled at me. I have been to many formal nights since and enjoyed every one of them, but never again did I have the duties of Mr Vice.

The remainder of my time at Army Office was to see me grow in confidence as a clerk and my Confidential Reports, a form that the Army used to monitor soldiers' progress, were glowing. It couldn't last however and there came a time when my boss told me that I needed to move on to further my career. I felt privileged that I was given an opportunity to make the change to Ordnance and even more so to be given a posting to Townsville on promotion to Staff Sergeant in the District Support Unit (DSU) at Laverack Barracks.

The time in Lyneham had taught me that there could be a balance between soldier and husband/father. It made me realise that Santa did leave presents at the end of kids' beds and that those same kids could be mischievous enough to steal lollies from the local shop and that they needed help to learn to ride those nice new pushbikes. There was still a lot of things that I had to learn about raising children, but they were to teach me all of those things as they grew up.

CHAPTER TWENTY-FIVE

OFF TO THE TROPICS

In May 1978 we departed our home in Lyneham and left for the new adventure in Townsville. The Army was very good at moving people and so I believed that it was going to be relatively pain-free to get to the new posting. In those days soldiers didn't take their furniture with them to Townsville but rather had it stored for them until their posting away from the tropics. The Department of Admin Services organised our pre- pack and uplift, and so we had only to pack our suitcases and move to a motel overnight and get to the airport the next morning, which was arranged for us.

I shall remember that day forever! There was a light frost in Canberra and so we rugged up with jumpers and slacks and jackets for the trip to Canberra Airport. It was the kids' first aeroplane trip and probably Pat's as well and so there was much excitement and perhaps a little nervous energy. The Army was good at organising movements, but this was my first attempt at getting a wife and four sprogs with all baggage from points a, b, c, d, and arriving unscathed at x, or at least as close as possible to it, without the aid of our car. Pat was far better qualified than I at these sorts of logistic exercises, having used the public system for shopping in Liverpool, but believing that I had some sort of leadership role, I assumed control and learned an extremely valuable lesson. The first part was to get us all in a taxi to the airport, and if it were in the days of compulsory seatbelts our journey would not have started. Pat had warned me about what should be packed and what should be carried but as leader I had overruled her and so we had this conglomeration of dolls, teddy bears, a bloody big monkey, and enough baggage to satisfy an African Safari. I knew then that this was going to be one helluva long day.

The family had come to see us off at the airport and there was much wailing, hugging, and gnashing of teeth as I, still believing that I was in control, checked tickets and departure times and where to go to change planes in Brisbane.

"Yes darling, you can take Monkey on the plane with you."

"But where will he sit, Daddy?"

"On his bottom, sweetheart."

"But he hasn't got a ticket, Daddy."

"I told you we should have packed him," Pat offered.

The call came to board the plane and luckily, we had two sets of three seats one behind the other but only two window seats. "I want the window," cried three children. Tim was too young to know about sibling rivalry yet.

Pat provided the correct solution with, "The two eldest can sit next to the window and then we'll change in Brisbane."

"How far is Bwisbun, Daddy?"

"Oh, it's a long way."

After a gentle taxi to the runway the excitement had grown to the point of requiring the use of a toilet.

"I told you to go before we got on!" I said.

"But I didn't want to go then," said our eldest.

"You'll have to wait until we are in the air because we are not allowed to stand up yet."

I'm sure that every parent has been through this diatribe but right then I was wishing that my posting was to Sydney or Albury or Wagga Wagga and not Townsville. We listened to the engines roar at the end of the runway and the plane started shaking and then hurtled off at breakneck speed and then Margaret and Robyn noticed that the distance between them and the ground was increasing at a great rate and that their tummies were still at ground level. I thought that they would be scared shitless but instead they, with the naivety of children, thought it was better than any show day ride that they had experienced. "Look how high we are!" and "Are those really the clouds Daddy?" and "How does the aeroplane stay in the sky?" and "Can we go to the toilet now, please?" I think that Pat was perhaps feeling the experience more than the rest of the family because she didn't want to remove her seatbelt and take the girls to the toilet and so the fearless leader was required to lead the procession backwards and forwards. The children loved this experience.

After another traumatic time changing planes in Brisbane, we finally came in to land at Townsville Airport. I don't know if things have changed at Townsville but in 1978 you had to walk from the plane to the terminal. Remember back to when we left Canberra and there was a slight frost and so we "rugged up", well we had also forgotten to take lighter clothing with us and as we stood in the doorway of the plane it was sweltering hot with humidity approaching one hundred percent, and we simply melted and flowed down the stairs. Pat declared that she was catching the next plane "home" and I stupidly pointed out that this was "home". Instant flashback to little Robin Hepple being told that he was going "home". Luckily, a happy smiling face approached us and after baggage collection we were taken straight to our motel overlooking the ocean, and lay in the air-conditioning and each thought our own thoughts of the impending three years of Townsville.

DEEP AND MEANINGFUL STUFF

When I had children and therefore the responsibility of raising them and yet not the knowledge of how to achieve this, I mistakenly thought that this also entailed some sort of ownership of the children. To allow them to develop their own personalities and prepare them for the next step in their lives, that of parenthood, I have come to realise that we cannot own children but rather simply guide and teach them as they become capable of understanding what you are imparting. At some point, they will want to become more responsible for their own actions but not the consequences of those actions, and we normally call this puberty or even pre-puberty, teens, or the period when they start to teach us about life.

I unfortunately never got that latter part in my upbringing and was given total autonomy to make mistakes but also to suffer the consequences alone. I was neither taught the right or wrong way to do anything and became quite selfish about the control of my life. This is in no way a "cop out" for the way in which my children have developed, and they must take a lot of that responsibility for themselves, barring medical intervention and physical appearance.

My need for ownership of my children's lives was only exceeded by Pat's, which is again how she was educated in her childhood and in this regard, we were and still are wrong. Our role should still be one of advisors and consolers.

I can now watch my grandchildren becoming young adults and still feel the need to overprotect and control their lives rather than allowing them to make decisions both good and bad and trying to guide and advise. My children no doubt have their own "methodology" for raising their children and I must become the relaxed Pop who is still fun to be around and a sympathetic ear when required. I would like to be around to see my great grandchildren develop their personalities.

CONCLUSION

This part of my story is now finished and my life will meander on to its inevitable conclusion in the company of my wonderful wife and my ever-aging family. If I was to reflect on the content of my life and ask the question "Why" then inevitably the answer would be simply "That's the way it happened." I can look back now and quite honestly say that I have, to date, enjoyed the majority of my time on this earth. I'm not a particularly clever person and have not contributed to the arts or sciences, nor have I produced anything of note that would change the inscription on my ultimate piece of masonry. But I have been a link in the never-ending chain of humanity and helped to perpetuate that chain into the future. Those cleverer than me will no doubt be able to analyse my life and put me in some definitive pigeonhole to leave me catalogued and filed away for future comparisons. But I believe that I am unique and that in the main it has been environment that has made me who I am.

There have been many emotions that I have experienced in my lifetime and most of them have made sense to me and do not leave me confused. There is one however that I cannot fully understand and probably never will. That emotion is LOVE. It is such a versatile word that it probably ranks right up there with the "F" word for its multitude of applications. "I love my dog", "I love my work", "I love some foods and some sports and some places", "I love my family and I have a special love for my wife", "I love to listen to rain on a tin roof on a cold and stormy night

203

when I am snuggled into my bed", "I love to ride a horse in the high country and feel the crisp chill mountain air in my face", "I love to go camping or fishing with my family or friends." The list is probably infinite but the meaning of the word love, as far as I can see, is simply the expression of feeling good to different degrees, of being comfortable and familiar with those and that which we love. Perhaps the test is in separation. I know from bitter experience that I have felt a physical sadness when separated from my wife and family, and I don't only mean geographically but in every sense of the word. A total detachment. I have heard that an analyst will ask if you loved your father and mother, and if they asked me, I would have to say no, because I didn't know them and I can't love someone that I don't know, and as such there have been times when my education in parenthood was lacking for the want of a role model—even a bad one might have helped.

During the time that I have been writing my story I have taken the opportunity to read several autobiographies and biographies. I have come to the conclusion that my life has not been as traumatic as many others and I would hate to think that you believe that I am bitter or remorseful in any way. I have asked my dear wife and my children to write short summaries of how they believe my life has affected them and I hope that they do and are totally honest in their appraisals.

Finally, I ask the question who or what is a Robin Clive Reed né Hepple. There are many adjectives that come to mind, such as introvert (almost anti-social), careful, logical, industrious, and reticent. But I doubt that we can be that uncomplicated, and therefore I think that my best description would be, "an outside person."